Gwen Sweetingham was born in Ilford Essex in 1944, lost her mother at five years old, and from a broken family, was raised to adulthood by her mother's six sisters, all of whose different lives and vibrantly contrasting personalities became hers to share. Their stories together are told in this book. After successful careers in nursing and women's fashion, she later married and turned her hand to property restoration in East Anglia. A life-long jazz lover, she is married to trumpeter, Digby Fairweather. This is her first book.

Seven Sisters

GWEN SWEETINGHAM

Seven Sisters

Vanguard Press

A CIP catalogue record for this title is
available from the British Library.

ISBN 978-1-80016-587-8

*Vanguard Press is an imprint of
Pegasus Elliot Mackenzie Publishers Ltd.*
www.pegasuspublishers.com

First Published in 2024

**Vanguard Press
Sheraton House Castle Park
Cambridge England**

Printed & Bound in Great Britain

To the seven sisters: Nell, Katie, Liddie, Jessie, Louisa, Mary and Ivy.

To Sheila

With my very
Best wishes

Gwen
xx.

With thanks to my husband Digby Fairweather for his encouragement and help in editing the text.

CHAPTER ONE

Ellen Fuller and her seven daughters: Ivy, Elizabeth,
Mary, Jessie, Louisa, Nellie, and Katie

These days, Seven Sisters is a bustling multicultural community in the London borough of Haringey. But before the Second World War, it was still part of the old London borough of Tottenham six miles from Ilford. If you wanted to travel from Seven Sisters to my first home at 165 Kingston Road Ilford, you could ride the old rumbling steam train from South Tottenham to Woodgrange Park, then walk the rest of the way. Or you could catch the bus, a ride of an hour or more. But for me, these two bustling London communities had something in common. Born into the heart of Ilford in 1944, I would be raised by another 'seven sisters'; all exhibiting the kind of girl-power that wouldn't be put into words for another sixty years. Their mother was Ellen Fuller and they were Nelly, Katy, Elizabeth, Jessie, Louisa, Mary and Ivy.

George Henry Fuller

Ellen, born in Wapping in 1870 had married George Henry Fuller when she was twenty years old and moved into the heart of Canning Town where industrial developments had moved at express pace and huge factories belched smoke and soot into the airs. George, a pipe-lagger died early from asbestosis but during a twenty-year marriage had fathered all seven sisters leaving Ellen to raise them by herself. A skilled seamstress she could survive by taking in work and find time to dress her daughters well. But life was tough and as well as learning to make do and mend at home, work had to be found for all her young daughters the minute they left school at fourteen. The older girls had to learn to take care of the younger ones too.

All seven had been born around the turn of the twentieth century in Canning Town; one of the roughest working-class areas anywhere in London. No more than half a century beforehand Canning Town didn't exist at all; there were only drab marshlands and saltings spilling over from the Thames spanned by rickety bridges. It was after the worst of the marshes were drained and the great Barking Road was opened that land became available for industrial business, and very soon homes for its workers would be needed too. In 1846 the North London train line arrived with a station to match, and most importantly the Royal Victoria Dock opened in 1855 providing manual labour for thousands of rough working men. A huge industrial development was rising in the Victorian age in a new location where manual labour was required and young men could find a job quickly.

But making lives for their wives and families was a tough challenge for these young men in Canning Town. Houses newly built for (or by) them turned into slums as soon as they were finished. Close to the river and well below high tide level, rising damp was an inevitability, and to make matters worse regular flooding from the Thames' filthy waters constantly spread disease and death from cholera, dysentery and smallpox. It was only after a full-scale cholera epidemic in 1855 that Canning Town, at last, had a clean water supply; before that its new arrivals could only drink yellow-green water from ditches poisoned by raw sewage which had to be boiled to make a cup of tea.

Canning Town (so said Charles Dickens), attracted 'offensive trade establishments; oil boilers, gut-spinners, varnish-makers, printers' ink makers and the like'. Building regulations there could be easily ignored by pirate landlords, labour was cheap and so, where necessary, was life. Silvertown, next door on the docks was every bit as dirty, with a pub on every corner (each one with a nickname of its own), and a great railway running along the docks crossed at one point by the 'peggy-leggy steps' which had no railings at all and where, it was said, a one-legged man had fallen to his death on the track below. Silvertown was a dangerous place to work anyhow; London's biggest-ever explosion happened in January 1917 during World War One when fifty tons of TNT blew up and seventy-three people were killed at the Brunner Mond munitions factory. But this was nothing compared to what had happened to their homes; seventy thousand damp and rickety buildings all over Canning town were either destroyed or badly damaged before anything at all which could be salvaged was patched up and put back together again, making an even bigger slum than before.

By 1910 however, nearly 300,000 people, including Ellen and her seven daughters, all lived in Canning Town, and despite its grimy surroundings, the community was a thriving hive of activity. There were more children than in any other London borough, as well as men and women from India, Malaysia, China, Japan and Germany, immigrants from all over Europe and the biggest black population anywhere in London. For a youngster, there was lots to be excited about in Canning Town too. All along the Barking Road, electric trams painted in vivid chocolate and cream took you to the grandly named Imperial Palace Theatre showing silent movies. There was a big public library, a recreation ground with a bandstand, a gymnasium and lido where people could swim, relax and pretend that they were lying on the beach thirty-five miles down the railway track at exotic Southend on Sea. For anyone with higher artistic or sporting aspirations, there was also the great four-storey Settlement House on the Barking Road. 'The Residence' as it was grandly called proudly hosted a boys' club, an orchestral society, a choral society, a dramatic society, a gymnastic society and clubs for rambling, cricket football and cycling. And then there was Rathbone Street Market where everybody did their shopping.

It was in this busy bustling working-class community that all seven sisters would grow up and by the time the Second World War came along in 1939 five of them had married — including my mother, Louisa Sweetingham.

CHAPTER TWO

My mother, Louisa

Of the seven sisters my mother Louisa was the third youngest, born in January 1910 in between Jessie, three years older and Mary, three years her junior. At the age of twenty-seven, she married James William Sweetingham in 1937 at Holy Trinity Church, Canning Town.

Louisa and James on their wedding day

James had been born in Canning Town in 1910 but altered his birth certificate so that he could join the Merchant Navy at seventeen instead of eighteen. He loved the sea, and Britain was still recovering from the First World War while the Great Depression of 1929 was just round the corner. So going to sea seemed like the best idea and James enlisted with the Port line, running out of London Docks, and sailing back and forth to India, Australia and New Zealand. As the round trip took twelve weeks, he was often away from his first home.

James Sweetingham

James hadn't enjoyed a happy childhood. No father was named on his birth certificate or, so far as he knew, for his two brothers John and Joe and his sister Sophie. So his single mother as well as being an alcoholic may have studied at the university of the world's oldest profession. His youngest sister Violet had also died unexpectedly in 1923 and when I was still very young I remember asking him about the tattoo with her name on his upper arm. Avoiding my gaze, his eyes glistened for the first time as he told me the story, and back in those 'boys don't cry' days the realisation that any man could weep was disturbing for a little girl.

James' first home had been in Hoy Street, Tidal Basin next to the Royal Docks. 'The Basin' as it was known, was the worst slum in Canning Town; finally levelled to earth forever in 1933 to make way for a viaduct across the Thames. His house was just like thousands of others, shabby and damp, with an outside lavatory, no hot water or central heating. So for years after he would wear the winceyette six-button vest under his shirt worn by most merchant naval men as something quite close to a uniform.

After he married Louisa, James gave up the sea and took a job at Beckton Gas Works; the largest in the world, and set, like the rest of Canning Town, in the grim ground-guzzling area of industrial London, deliberately shifted away to the east of the city by the refined residents of Mayfair. Nearby to Beckton was the gigantic Tate and Lyle factory co-owned by Henry Tate and Abram Lyle, and just as daunting, the old offices of the Thames Ironwork and Shipbuilding Company; a forbidding leviathan straddling the rough lands around Bow Creek and dominating its smoky landscape. All these old buildings were black with grime and coal-soot and workmen at Beckton had a building where they would throw off their working clothes and shower after their shifts; there was nowhere to get clean quickly at home. Less than a year after their wedding James and Louisa had a son, James Edward — known from the very beginning as Jimmy.

Louisa and son Jimmy

To begin with, they had moved in with Louisa's sister Elizabeth (always called 'Liddie'), in Canning Town but this quickly turned into a problem. James' new wife was asthmatic and as well as Beckton other chemical companies and foul-smelling industries left the air heavy with industrial smoke and waste; a big threat to anyone with asthma.

So very soon James decided to move away from Canning Town to Ilford five miles away. There his wife could breathe in comfort; there would be nicer surroundings to bring up their children and life would be better. Ilford, James reckoned, would be quite different to Canning Town. It was a pleasant suburb on the Essex borders with pavements rather than broken-down mud tracks, roads with proper street lighting and all but devoid of traffic, and no less than twenty five landscaped parks. For sure his wife should be all right there.

The house they rented at 165 Kingston Road, Ilford was just one more of hundreds in terraced rows and of identical red brick design; a slate roof, three bedrooms with high ceilings and sash windows and built before the turn of the century. Drive down Kingston Road and you can still see it today.

But back then their house was not that much different from James' first home in Canning Town. Its rooms were still lit by gas — some of their neighbours didn't have electricity connected until after the Second World War — and if you struck a match anywhere near an unguarded mantle flames shot up to the ceiling. The one and only toilet was outside; there was no hot water system and no central heating. And if you needed a bath it was in the scullery — not many people remember sculleries these days — with a boiler beside it. In this tiny room at the back of the house where dishes were washed or dirty household chores finished, you lit the fire under the boiler, waited for the water to heat up and then used a bucket to pitch the water into the bath. But the bath was metal, not enamel, and slipping down into the water could take the skin off your back.

Eighteen months after Jimmy was born, along came World War Two and Louisa, her new husband and son faced what were then unspeakable terrors. So did Louisa's six sisters back in Canning Town. London's East End was mercilessly bombed for fifty-six days and nights and of all its boroughs Canning Town came off quite the worst; ninety-six bombs rained down on its hapless population between October 1940 and June 1941. All of the young women somehow survived, but Nell and Liddie would lose their husbands in industrial accidents along London's docks, decades before the words 'health and safety' had been thought of.

Liddie and her first husband killed in World War I

Amid the bombs the young women would still be expected to get into work after catastrophic night raids, dodging still-smouldering craters and putting up with bus drivers struggling to stick to their routes and stops, despite the remains of bombed-out houses and tumbling masonry. Aunt Mary would put her umbrella up as protection against falling brickwork as she tramped her way to Standard Telephones in Silvertown; another of the East End areas to suffer worst from the raids. Food was very difficult to find in London too; there were thousands of big families like Mary's and queuing to use your ration coupons at the store — if it happened to be still there — was an everlasting chore. All seven girls took it in turns to do the errands and take the risks too.

As soon as war was declared however Louisa and Jimmy were evacuated to Somerset for the 'phony war' from September 1939 to April 1940 when, after Hitler's *blitzkrieg* attack on Poland, he seemed to have forgotten about London completely. Both of them were sent away anyhow, to be on the safe side, and Jimmy's first memory was his mother screaming in horror at the sight of rats running in the barns around the country farm which was their designated home. So back to Ilford they came. The threat of bombing raids was still so feared however that, like thousands of London children Jimmy, at just three years old, was to be sent to Canada or Australia for the duration. For him, the choice was Australia, a voyage of six weeks, and the preliminary was an assembly on London Docks for a quick dental check where any problem teeth were hastily pulled out by unfeeling dentists. However, just before departure, a message came through; the previous ship bound for Australia had been torpedoed and the crew and children had either been killed or drowned.

So it was decided that the family would stay together whatever the risks and James made up his mind to build an Anderson shelter. It arrived in three or four corrugated iron sections which he bolted together after digging as deep a hole as he could in the garden; then piled earth on the top of the shelter for extra protection. The Sweetingham trio dutifully trooped down to it whenever the sirens began to ululate their terrifying warnings in the early days of the war until they got tired of the routine.

But then the real London blitz arrived, and one night Jimmy and Louisa ignored the sirens once too often. Minutes later they were thrown out of their bedroom and into the garden amid the bricks and rubble as the explosion blew the back wall of their house apart. After that they slept downstairs in their sitting room until the second bomb came down in 1944 next door to their home. They survived again but Jimmy remembered walking about in a daze with his legs burning. The explosion had blown hot soot down from the chimney above the open fire which burned in the fireplace every winter. So after that Jimmy, now five years old, was evacuated again to Dunstable to stay with Nell, the eldest of the seven sisters.

After the Blitz Ilford was still close enough to East London for German bombers to get rid of their cargo, and these included incendiary bombs; smaller affairs intended to set fire to the building they landed on. As a result, rather than waiting for the bomb disposal unit to turn up, civilians were encouraged to deal with them on their own, using sand, a mat or whatever came to hand. If they landed on slate roofs on nearby houses, young James was up to the challenge; he'd regularly scale a ladder with a broom and a pair of thick leather gloves to bring down the bombs before they did any damage.

In March 1944, as well as the war, the Sweetingham family faced an additional challenge: my arrival as their one and only daughter. By then the war was in its last year, and one of my first memories is riding on the miniature saddle which James had attached behind him on his bicycle as he rode steadily along the roads running errands. It was fun to see his neighbours shopping or trimming their hedges; he would call 'hello' to anyone he knew and they would call back and wave. So, it seemed to me, that my father was a well-liked cheerful soul who got on with people. And day by day I was learning to love him more.

But Beckton Gas Works seemed a long way away to me and I often would miss his presence at home. James worked in eight-hour shifts; two in the afternoon to ten at night; ten at night to six in the morning, or six in the morning to two in the afternoon. This meant that he sometimes slept the day away, and I would have to play quietly around the house. But if the weather was warm and sunny my mother would walk me to the Ilford parks. We'd wander around the lakes, watch the ducks and swans, and I could ride the swings and roundabouts. So my father couldn't always be with me. But my mother was — and for now, that was all that mattered.

CHAPTER THREE

My mother's name was Louisa, she was always called 'Louie' at home, and I adored her. One of my earliest memories is the sight and sound of her sitting at her old treadle Singer sewing machine. She had learned her mother's lessons well and was a skilled seamstress who made all my childhood clothes at home. Money was tight but she managed to find fabric every time, even though I was growing fast and soon needed the next size up. So Louie made sure that there was always plenty of hem to let down. I'd watch as she'd lay out the material on our dining room table, pin the paper patterns on and then cut the cloth around them. Everything was organised with set procedures; I could see how it all came together. I thought my mother was a marvel but had no idea that this was one of the first lessons that, sooner not later, I would need to learn for myself.

In our primitive kitchen at 165 Kingston — just an old gas stove, a big Butler sink and a few hooks on the wall for saucepans — Louie's cooking skills were tested to their limit and meals for two adults and two children must have been a challenge. But she took it all in her womanly stride. Tall and slim with dark curly hair she always had a joyful smile ready for me and the world, and I thought she looked pretty and smartly turned out in her homemade dresses as we walked hand in hand down our long road to the bus stop. Louie never used baby-talk but would chat to me like a grown-up, and stop along the way too when neighbours said, "good morning." There would be more talk about the bombs and whom they had missed (or otherwise), the children, the price of meat and the eternal grumbles about post-war food rationing and ration books. But I was always the centre of kind Louie's attentions. One very cold day we were walking briskly along the road when my tall mother stopped to bend down to my face. "Can I hear your teeth chattering?" she asked. "Then we'd better hurry up to get home."

Sometimes when my father was working a day shift Louie would take me back over to Canning Town where sisters Liddie, Katy, Ivy and Mary were still living after the bombs had stopped. The trolley bus ride to nearby Barking was memorable, especially — at least for me — if the electric connectors of the bus came off the overhead cables. This happened a lot and the conductor would have to use a long pole to re-attach them; a trick which some of them were good at, others not. So it might take several tries (and quite a lot of fruity language) before we were ready to go again. Then we'd change at Barking and get on the motor bus, a noisier jerkier journey through East Ham and then on and into Canning Town. Though there was still bomb damage all round, the streets were full of life and enterprising locals had set up stalls and small businesses on the sites.

At Canning Town, we'd walk from Hermit Road to Durham Road where grandmother Ellen Fuller still lived on the ground floor at number thirty-five with Aunt Ivy and husband John in the next room. By now she was ill and died soon after; perhaps the challenge of bringing up seven siblings on her own had at last worn her away. I wish I'd had time to know her better.

On these trips my first-ever streaks of envy were seeing two little boys, on equally tiny bikes, racing each other around a local park. So far, my only set of wheels had been a scooter but I knew straight away that I wanted a bike of my own. However, at Christmas when I was three years old, disaster; I woke up to find a doll's pram by the bed. I really didn't want this at all but did my level best to look pleased; dolls' prams cost money. I simply couldn't see the point of putting a doll in a pram and pushing it around. But I was a girl and therefore automatically expected to be interested in babies, and one day motherhood too. This was 1947 and times were different.

However, on my fourth birthday three months later a big surprise: the pram disappeared and here was a tricycle.

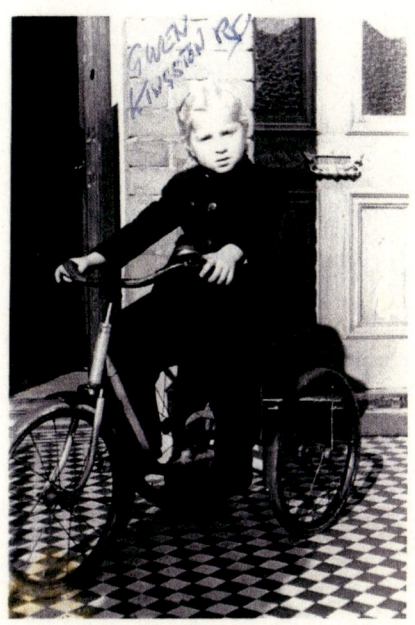

Probably my parents had seen through my attempts to look grateful. But now I couldn't wait to get to the park and race about on my very first — though certainly not my last — set of wheels. I could join my young friends Johnny and Alan in the park fully mobilised, and even ride on the Ilford roads too; there was no traffic around.

But I outgrew my tricycle equally quickly and one birthday later, a real two-wheeler arrived. So at five years old I could join eleven-year old Jimmy and his chums on bigger adventures in junk shops and on bomb sites, and very soon was every bit as mucky as my big brother. I had to learn to take care of my bike too, and one lesson I learned early on was to boil its chain in engine oil on the kitchen stove in our frying-pan, (luckily Louie knew when we'd done it); then hang it on the garden fence to cool. This was the best way to make sure the chain worked smoothly and if it came off anyhow, I had to learn for myself how to put it back on, as well as change worn brake-rubbers and even mend a puncture. Back then, poor as we were, everything was repaired rather than replaced — recycling in every sense and in its earliest form. So I was a tomboy, but happy to be, as none of the girls I knew wanted to join our adventures.

On Saturdays Jimmy would take me to the pictures at the Regal Cinema in Ilford High Road. The Regal was part of the big ABC chain and every Saturday morning it was packed with hundreds of noisy children to watch cartoons, Laurel and Hardy, Abbott and Costello, Roy Rogers and Trigger, Hopalong Cassidy, and Pathé' children's newsreels. We all joined the club known, for some reason, as the ABC Minors. But we didn't mind being 'Minors'; that didn't make us feel inferior. After all, we were each given a badge

and our own theme-song to sing to the tune of *Blaze Away*:

> 'We are the boys and girls well known as
> The Minors of the ABC
> And every Saturday we line-up
> And see the films we like to see and shout aloud with glee
> We like to laugh and have a singsong
> Such a happy crowd are we!
> We're all pals together
> We're the Minors of the ABC!'

When the line about 'shout aloud with glee' came along we were encouraged to do exactly that and it's amazing that the roof of the Regal wasn't raised in the process. No doubt we were a rowdy bunch but Jimmy won a bigger badge than me as he was appointed a 'minor monitor' in charge of keeping rows of children in order. It never worked at all, but probably Jimmy had free tickets in exchange for his monitor's duties and it was more honest than 'bunking in'.

Then came my first day at Woodlands Infant School in Ilford. It was only a short walk, and Louie held my hand on the way. She also came into the classroom to meet my teacher, Miss Moffat. But I never noticed when she left because there was so much to take in; lots of other children to make friends with, a mysterious blackboard behind the teacher's desk, and dozens of new exciting books lining the shelves. And everything was small too; tiny chairs and desks and in the toilet block across the hall mini-toilets and basins. So, when Louie came to call for me after school I couldn't stop talking about my day and remember her laughter as she remembered that I'd been nervous when we left home in the morning. As she tucked me into bed that evening she asked if I wanted to go to school now? Of course I did, and my mother was happy.

My first school portrait

I also acquired my first autograph book from Aunt Jessie who by now had moved from Canning Town with her husband Albert and lived in the same street as us, Kingston Road at number 251. All my aunts had to sign my book, and my teachers too, but it was Albert, my favourite uncle of all, who signed with a flourish and an ode to accompany his signature:

In days of old, when knights were bold

And paper wasn't invented,

They wiped their arse on blades of grass

And went away contented!

Quite an adult dedication for a five-year old, and it was the first time I'd seen demure Jessie roar with laughter. But behind her reserved exterior there was a hearty cockney sense of humour along with that strong steel spirit. And as my life went along it was Jessie — of all seven sisters — who would come back again and again; to help me, to rescue me, and later to guide me in adult matters where no one else wanted to help. As we shall see, in her own quiet way, Aunt Jessie would be my first and last saviour.

For now though, in our four-piece family, life was good. It seemed to me that the sun shone every day in a blue sky and I was growing up to be an optimist whose glass, then as now, has always been half full, never half empty. Songs I heard back then on the radio like *On the Sunny Side of the Street*, *Keep your Sunny Side Up* and *When You're Smiling* made me smile too and sing along. I watched my mother at her sewing machine, fed our chickens in the back yard and played with the neighbourhood boys. A bomb site just around the corner was a nearby attraction for we Ilford juniors and we called it 'the wildo'. But on the site weeds and wild flowers had sprung up where houses had so recently stood — nature's benign response to trauma, tragedy and death.

We had a tidy home too. Everything in the house had its place, including toys for my brother and me. If we played with them, we were told to put them back right away afterwards in our toy cupboard. It became automatic to do this; no chore and we always knew where something was when we wanted it.

I was also learning to read, and very quickly. Back then I wanted to read everything. In my schoolbooks I discovered places and people far away, and adventure stories which made me long for new ones of my own. Back at home my mother or father were always nearby; sometimes the two of them were at home together too. And Jimmy who was growing up fast would amaze me with his Meccano set, building complex machines that raised, lowered or rotated obediently at his command when he switched on a tiny electric motor.

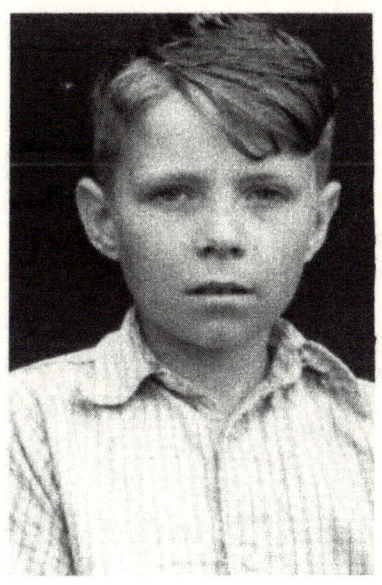

Young Jimmy

Jimmy was always occupied: building or repairing anything from a clock to a bicycle that he found on a junk heap or swapped with his pals. And as money was a constant issue he would bring his damaged acquisition back to life, then sell it for cash. Another way to raise money was to chip lead off our drainpipe, melt it down and drop it into the moulds he had made to produce tiny lead soldiers which he'd sell at school. Once Jimmy had brought an old banjo home with the idea of learning to play, but couldn't make head or tail of the instrument. But Aunt Liddie's husband, Billie, was a tough customer, and he earned cash of his own playing the banjo in local pubs.

When he heard about Jimmy's find, Billy called in to make a bid, but his offer wasn't good enough and our uncle went home empty-handed. A week later however he called back with a much better price and this time Jimmy took it; the best profit he had ever made. My father was envious. "I'd have to work a week to make money like that," he said.

Another of Jimmy's more spectacular retrievals was a false leg, in the days when such limbs were made to look as lifelike as possible. He must have found it in a junk shop or on a bomb site but home it came and turned up just about anywhere; in a cupboard covered by a towel, in a bed, or to give someone a turn. It always worked particularly well with girlfriends who he'd pick up for a date in his latest car. Slipping into the front seat they'd spot it leisurely draped over the back seat breaking the ice, one way or another, from the start.

Very quickly I was able to join Jimmy and his friends at the grown-up cinemas too; the infamous 'Bug'Ole' opposite the police station in Ripple Road Barking and 'Fleapit' in Ilford High Road. But I knew that these young mens' other interests as they developed were still far more exciting than anything my girlfriends wanted to talk about. First came speedway bicycles, then motor bikes, then cars. None of them were in working order when they arrived at our home but Jimmy would set about putting them right without spending any of his hard-earned cash. This meant trips to the local breaker's yard for spare parts and very quickly I could see my brother turning into a fine young engineer.

One of the few luxuries Louie had at Kingston Road was an early Hoover vacuum cleaner; a heavy beast with a black cloth dust collection bag, ceremoniously parked in our front room. Most households still had a Ewbank carpet sweeper, but there was a reason for this expensive addition to our home; Louie wouldn't need to sweep the carpet, stirring up the dust. We still had a coal fire but because of the smoke which made her asthma worse, it was only lit as a last resort on the coldest days and nights. So there were times when the house was chilly and we had to 'wrap up' to keep warm. But though we were poor, we were happy. The war was over and done with; there were good times waiting, and a new sun in the sky.

CHAPTER FOUR

But outside in the airs of Ilford, when the sun didn't shine, there were still the legendary London smogs to face and to breathe; a horrid health menace which spread far beyond Canning Town and all across London. Smog was a combination of the smoke and gases which poured into the air from the countless chimneys, houses and factories in and beyond London's East End, producing 'pea-soupers'; the feared dense, yellow-tinged fogs which, before the UK Government's Clean Air Act in 1956, forced their way into your nose and down your throat whenever you left the house. And if there was no windy weather the smog could hang in the air for days. For anyone with chest problems, they were a dangerous menace, and not about to blow away. The London smog disaster in 1952 claimed around 12,000 lives in London in just four days, including thousands of cab drivers who drove through the toxic airs day by day and even had a special cough mixture — called 'Cabdriver'; an early example of focussed marketing — to try and clear their chests. But even keeping their windows tightly closed couldn't get rid of the problem and many of them died.

Although Louie and James had moved to Ilford to be further away from the pollution all around Canning Town, the relocation did nothing to help my mother once a peasouper arrived. Then her asthma would take a sudden frightening turn, and she would be rushed to hospital again. But the medication she was given had no effect when she arrived back home. When she became pregnant with her daughter in 1943 it worsened again and there were yet more trips to King George's hospital in Ilford where I would be born in March 1944.

But my arrival did nothing to send the peasoupers away. They kept on relentlessly arriving and worsening and the winter of 1949 seemed to start early and carry on remorselessly. And with it back came the smog. At Woodlands school, less than a quarter of a mile away, I was five years old now and still only vaguely aware that sometimes my mother was ill. I still enjoyed my lessons and new friends, and if she couldn't take me I could walk to school by myself. But as the weather worsened my mother's health did the same, and once again I knew that she had been taken back into hospital. Ever-faithful cautious Aunt Jessie, only forty-three doors away in Kingston Road, began collecting me from school most days, carrying umbrellas and extra clothing 'just in case' of rain or more snow in the freezing streets. It was nice to have my aunt walk home with me or be invited back to her house for tea. But by December this was happening much more often. And somehow the cold weather and my mother's illness put a new chill of fear in the air, and into our family too.

School broke up for the Christmas holidays on December 20th, my father's fortieth birthday. But despite the unspoken fears I was still looking forward to Christmas Day, the presents I was hoping for, and our family's usual big get-together on Boxing Day at Aunt Liddy's house. We'd eat and drink; there would be a Christmas tree with tiny gifts and Christmas crackers, and everyone, including Uncle Billy and his banjo would do a turn singing their favourite song round Liddy's upright piano. If my father was on his afternoon shift, from two to ten he would turn up late, play the piano with more enthusiasm than skill, sing songs and get things going with his stories and jokes; he had always been the life of any party.

But this year he wouldn't be there at all. I wasn't allowed into Louie's bedroom, saw more and more of Jessie, and one day quite unexpectedly was collected from Ilford by my Aunt Mary; taken back to Canning Town and told that I would be staying there for a while. Christmas seemed far removed now and my presents including a tiny handbag had been wrapped up before being sent over to Mary's house for me to open. But there were no festivities, no tree and no Boxing Day party. My father didn't come to Mary's house; Christmas came and went with nothing to celebrate and eventually I was taken home.

By now my mother was nowhere to be seen; Jessie began calling at our house more and more, and I would go with her on shopping trips to Ilford. But now she didn't seem her normal self at all; brother Jimmy was unusually quiet and my father, so it seemed, had gone back to work. And then, on one more bitterly cold day, it was arranged for me to stay with neighbours over the road while our house looked to be empty. So where had everybody gone? Later Jimmy came to collect me and when we came back through the door, I was surprised to find several family members in the room: all of them quiet and some of them red-eyed. But surely, I thought, it must have been the frozen air outside that made their eyes water.

Then it was time for school again. Jessie took me on the first day of term, and I couldn't understand why she took time to speak to Miss Moffat; she had never spoken to my teacher before. But life carried on; I was beginning to wonder seriously when I would see my mother again, but nobody wanted to answer my questions. Of course it was a difficult thing to explain to a child. But the fact was that my mother had died on December 27th, 1950, and it had been her funeral on the day I'd been sent over to my neighbours and come back to find everyone tearful.

Then one night after I had gone to bed my father came in to say goodnight and it was time for my question to receive its answer.

"Where is Mum and when is she coming home?" I asked. My father was silent for a long time.

"Where do you think she is?" he asked.

"I don't know Dad," I said. "Is she still in hospital?"

"No," said my father. "What else do you think?"

The conversation was taking a dark turn, but somehow I found the words.

"Has Mum died?" My father's three words came quickly.

"Yes, she has," he said.

My brain went blank. I hadn't believed this could happen and for moments I was speechless. Then as the shock sank in I felt sick, giddy and lost, and began to cry. My father stayed and slept with me that night, but from now on nights with their horrid dreams became things to fear; I would wake up screaming and began to wet the bed. Jessie, who had no children of her own, would stay overnight too so that she could be there for me, but the nightmares continued and I became scared of the dark for the first time. James briefly stopped his night shifts, even though he was paid more for them so that he could be with me when Jessie went home to Uncle Albert, but there was nothing more either of them could do.

It was no surprise that I hadn't been told about my mother's death or her funeral. Back then young children were generally spared the gloomy ceremony. So I would only gradually find out that when my mother had died at forty years old from an asthma attack, she had been in the bedroom with only my father to comfort her at her side. He had first had to witness her last pitiable moments and departure, then go out in the freezing days with their long black nights when all the offices and shops were closed for Christmas to somehow register her death and find an undertaker in order to arrange her funeral which had taken place early in January 1951.

All of this information had been kept from me. But now Aunt Jessie was in our house much of the time; her bereaved brother-in-law had no idea how to cope with a small daughter and young son. She had sewn the emblematic black triangle of mourning on the upper arm of his jacket and one for Jimmy too as he was twelve years old and just about ready to face the facts of death. But I was still too young and when I had asked about the black triangles there had been no answer again.

So our once happy family was derailed now and life could never be the same. James had lost both his wife and his life's way, and as the long desperate winter wore on, he began to drink away his sorrow at 'The Plough' in Ilford Lane on his way back from Beckton. He had always enjoyed drinking; as a merchant seaman during the war he'd caroused happily in endless taverns during stopovers at ports in Australia, New Zealand and South America. But now drink wasn't a social pleasure but a nightly necessity, and all too soon we were to find out that poor lonely James Sweetingham, once in his cups, would let his grief out in an evil temper; something I had never seen before. It was a terrifying revelation too. Uncouth, loud and aggressive he became Hyde, not Jekyll and the father I had known and loved mysteriously defocused then disappeared within weeks. He would pick on his son, now twelve years old and growing up fast, and shouting rows between the two of them began. They frightened me and I wanted them to stop but didn't know how.

Quickly though my aunts, as well as my father realized the situation. So, full of depression, remorse and the first anger of bereavement James was forced to realise that his daughter was just one child too many. So he would take me to Aunt Mary's house in Addington Road, Canning Town on Friday night to keep me out of the way of what he knew all too well would break out at home. Away from the fear, the rows and raised voices, Mary would cook good food for me and I would stay until Sunday evening when she would bring me home ready for school the next day.

But now from a happily united family foursome, we had turned within weeks into a torn apart trio of unhappy individuals. Something had to be done, and quickly.

CHAPTER FIVE

So my father and his six sisters-in-law put their seven heads together and came to a family decision: a housekeeper had to be found for Kingston Road. An advertisement was placed in the local newspaper and a series of women arrived at our house to be interviewed.

Once again it was Aunt Jessie who was on hand; my beleaguered father needed help to find the housekeeper he would never have dreamed of needing a year before.

Aunt Jessie when young

For Jessie, interviewing strange women to care for her favourite sister's children must have been nothing less than heart-breaking; she had been in the house when Louie had drawn her last despairing breath and my mother had been her favourite sister. At school, bespectacled shy young Jessie had been called 'four-eyes' and spunky young Louie, three years her junior, would stand up to bullies that threatened her and send them packing.

So these reluctant meetings to find a housekeeper took a long time. I didn't like the look of any of the applicants either and hoped that none of them would ever come to live with us. Perhaps, I thought, things might gradually improve. I also noticed that if I didn't do things around our once spit-spot clean house they wouldn't be done at all now, so, although I was still too small to man the vacuum cleaner, dusting became part of my daily routine. When I stayed with Mary at weekends, she also began to teach me how to cook simple meals, and how to wash undies and hang them on the washing line to dry. She realised that I was going to need to know about the necessities of life now, and although I found it hard at first, with Mary's help I was able to master some of her simpler household skills. Not so much time for playing now.

After what seemed to be an endless queue of interviewees one was eventually hired. Her name, was Rose and we were told, she would be moving very soon. She had a young son Graham too, so she would need the largest bedroom in the house; the one where my father and mother had once slept peacefully side by side, but where he had also watched her die. I was to sleep with my father in our second bedroom unless he was on his night shifts, and Jimmy would continue to sleep in our tiniest bedroom next door to the two of us.

Up until then Rose, who told her interviewers she was a widow, had been living in a one-bedroom flat at the top of an old slum building in Canning Town. She had no doubt decided that the job of housekeeper in up-market Ilford would solve her housing problem and provide somewhere better to raise her young son. So, the day came for her to make her move, and in she came with all her luggage and four-year old Graham; two years younger than me. But her arrival was nothing compared to her son's which seemed more like a destructive tornado; running all over our once-tidy home, Graham seemed to turn it into a shambles within minutes. I had never seen anything like it and wondered why my father, Aunt Jessie — or our new housekeeper — didn't bring this feral force of nature to heel. This was the end of our ordered way of life and privacy; our home, it seemed, was abruptly and inexplicably given over to a pair of strangers to turn it into whatever they wanted, and I hated and feared everything.

Nothing could have been more awkward. As the days went by my father was afraid of saying anything to young Graham to calm him down for fear of upsetting his new housekeeper; a woman he barely knew. In turn, Rose had no intention at all of making friends with the young people in her new household. And as the days turned into weeks and months, it seemed, however unbelievably, that she was somehow turning into our surrogate mother. If something went wrong, she quickly became more personally intrusive, and if she felt we'd misbehaved, out — however inappropriately — would come the age-old threat: 'wait 'till your father gets home!' When he did, the tales she told James about our perceived misdoings were elaborated beyond belief and arguments would break out between the two of them; my father knew that we were not bad children. But Rose who was cleverer with words than her employer was always able to shout him down. So very soon there was no getting away from it; we were living in a broken home. My brother's life became more difficult still and I realised that I could never do anything to please our new housekeeper. So I withdrew into my own world with my books. I read and read and then read more — taking on board adventure stories, boy's tales and also sentimental tales of family life like 'Little Women' with their happy endings which now seemed so far away.

But it was less than a year later in 1952, when I was just eight years old, that a new peacetime bombshell struck our home. Rose and my father had gone out together on their own one day, and when they returned with cheery flowers in their buttonholes, we were told that they were married. I was dumbfounded and there would be more changes now. The two of them would move into the second bedroom to sleep together. I would move into the front bedroom and into the bed where my father and mother had so recently slept together while Graham would sleep in a single bed next to me. Jimmy would stay where he was and we were both baldly told to call Rose 'Mum'. But this was one step too far. I missed my mother more than I could say; she had died far too recently and this was one order I simply could not keep. Rather than trying to understand the situation however my new stepmother decided to add it to my supposed list of sins. So the stories of her newly and officially adopted stepchildren's misdemeanours carried more weight than ever, as they were remorselessly delivered, night by night, to her reluctant, often wordlessly resigned husband.

In short we were not wanted, and three years later a new baby would arrive pushing us even further away. My father had consecrated his new love by producing a daughter with his second wife, so there was less room than ever for the children he had fathered with his first. Jimmy would make his own lonely way into his teenage years. And my six aunts — seven sisters minus one — would need to step in to teach me about life, how to grow up, and most important of all, how to be loved.

CHAPTER SIX

Of course it was shy kind Aunt Jessie who had been the first to be a central part of our lives. Living in Kingston Road it was easy for her to be there; dropping into our house every day, and more regularly still to see Louie as her sister's asthma had worsened. Often, at the end, my mother had been too ill to go shopping at all; Jessie took over and I would go along with her for the trip. Like my mother, she seemed to know lots of people in the neighbourhood and was also a careful shopper considering her purchases thoughtfully before each transaction. So, every trip could take some time. She would take me into the sweet shop too, giving up her precious post-war ration to her five-year old niece. My choice would always be 'flying saucers'; sherbet wrapped in rice paper which exploded in your mouth when the paper melted. Respectable Jessie would always try to persuade me to choose something else; she considered my flying saucers a poor substitute for what she termed 'proper sweeties'. But I was allowed to make up my own mind and got my way before we went back to her house for tea.

Jessie

Like my mother, Jessie was tall, walked down the street in an upright manner, and would never leave the house unless she was, in her own words, 'bandbox fresh'. My aunt could come out with such marvellous phrases, and for her, this would mean a fresh dress every day, a smart coat (she had three) with hats to match, gloves and fashionable shoes. Every time she took me to see her sisters, she would make sure that I was 'bandbox fresh' too. But I didn't have a second set of clothes so she would freshen-up what I was wearing to make sure that I didn't show up as a mucky kid.

Jessie and her husband, Herbert Ramsey, had been engaged for seven long years. For the whole of their marriage Herbert had been called 'Albert' instead, and when I asked why Jessie explained that back in London's East End if somebody was stupid, they would be called a 'right Herbert'. So Albert was better. When he was feeling affectionate to his wife Albert had a nickname for his wife too; he would call her 'Jessums'.

Jessie and Albert

When I asked why it had taken so long for the two of them to marry she explained that it was because Albert had found it impossible to get any kind of steady job in

Canning Town. Even in this huge working-class community unemployment had struck hard in the 1930s depression years, and the marriage was postponed time and time again as one job after another came to an end. So the engagement ring was returned (or, so said her sisters, occasionally thrown back!) more than once or twice by the disappointed bride; Jessie could dispense with her propriety for special occasions. Finally, they decided to marry anyway; almost immediately Albert found permanent employment and the young couple managed to gather enough money to put down a deposit for a small house in Canning Town where they settled down, just in time for World War Two.

Albert and Jessie on their wedding day

But they were quickly bombed out and thereafter moved to 251 Kingston Road choosing to rent their new home for the next forty years until Albert died. Why was this? They were a simple couple and worried that the Germans might come back and bomb them again.

In Jessie's case, this naïvety extended into their bedroom too. When she married Albert, she had had no idea what sex was all about, and her embarrassed husband had to find a book to tell her about the basics. This was quite a problem and challenge; back in the early 1930s there were no manuals explaining or celebrating the happy and glorious acts of love, and many people had no idea what to do with their feelings, or even where to put what if they had them. There was even a movie in 1941 called *Six lessons from Madam La Zonga* starring Lupe Velez which turned up later as a spoof sex manual for Bob Hope in the movie *The Road to Singapore* with Bing Crosby. Presumably, Albert and Jessie managed to conquer their problems somehow but they never had children. And over the years I became more and more aware that Jessie saw me as her surrogate daughter; a role which — more than any of my other aunts — she would continue to play for life.

On my third Christmas, still a tiny girl with no boyish aspirations, I had been given a doll's house. Using an old breadboard as the base, my father had built and painted the frame and its rooms, and my mother had made tiny curtains and bed linen.

But it was Albert who made most of the furniture to go inside. So, in the following weeks, miniature chairs and tables for the dining room and beds for the bedrooms arrived and gradually I became the proud owner of a fully furnished house. Watching it grow week by week I was getting my first lessons in home decorating and furnishing; something useful for me in future years.

As a special treat, I could watch Jessie make fairy cakes and was soon allowed to join in. Even better than the fun was the smell of the cakes as they baked; my own first batch coming out of the oven, and the impatient waiting while they cooled down. But Jessie would also make the point that we mustn't eat all the tiny cakes ourselves; sharing between families was the proper thing to do. This was difficult — the cakes were hard to resist — but it was one of life's lessons I would learn early on from my aunt. Always very proper she would also gently correct me if she thought that I was behaving badly, getting cheeky or uppity. 'Best not do that' she would quietly remind me (another favourite phrase), and there were many times that it would make me stop and think. But if she thought I'd said something beyond the ordinary her expression was different. "You're a clever little cock sparra," she'd say, reverting to her cockney roots for once, and I'd feel special.

So Jessie was the first to teach me the basics of good manners. Always thoughtful and kind to me as well as everyone else, she loved to tell me stories about grandmother, Ellen Fuller. And if I wanted to know anything at all about my own mother Louie, her sisters and their childhood she was the one to ask; as three of her siblings were older than her and three younger, she was poised to remember her childhood times from both directions.

Jessie would remain an unobtrusive but ever-present supporter in my childhood. Later in my teenage years, she would make another dramatic re-entry at my life's most traumatic point so far. And even later she would help me to rationalise and resolve one of my most difficult decisions of all. For all of her years, Aunt Jessie Ramsey would remain my most unobtrusive yet constant guardian angel.

But it was the second eldest of the sisters Katy who would open my eyes to more great things as I began to grow.

CHAPTER SEVEN

Katy's house in Star Lane, Canning Town, was set even further back in time than any of her other sisters. Her scullery still had its concrete boiler for washing clothes, and a cast-iron Victorian kitchen range always had something promising cooking in its oven and a kettle boiling on its hob to make tea for every visitor. Food was always an important part of her family's life; a welcome change from the near-starvation regime now in operation, back home at 165 Kingston Road. She'd cook delicious stews and apple pies and buckets of custard to go with them.

Katy was never the most smartly turned out of her sisters, but when she was young, she had been beautiful. And though later her healthy appetite had turned her into a big woman she was warm, welcoming, and always ready to greet her young guest with hugs and a cuddle. And these had begun as soon as she had heard about my troubles at home. Radiating inner peace and well-being she never seemed to be worried or upset about anything at all and could, so it seemed, glide over problems smoothing them over as they arrived. She was a thinker too; kind and considerate of other peoples' feelings and would always include me in talks about grown-up family matters, asking questions that I had to think about before I could answer. These would include the difficult matter of my troubled father after he had lost his wife and turned to drink; how was young James and was he still riding his motor bike? All of the sisters had liked my father; knew he was suffering after my mother's death and that things weren't easy at home. But it was only Katy who made a point of asking about James Sweetingham and his first family, now so wilfully torn apart.

She would also be the one to ask me what I was reading now; was I enjoying it, how far had I got, and what was next on the list? There was a reason for this; Katy's house was full of books. They were everywhere; piled on any free space, and quite often on the floor too. She had been clever at school, but had had to leave as soon as possible to earn money for her mother and six sisters. So books had been acquired every which way over the years; some new, some second-hand, some gifts. And if she ran out of reading, Katy could walk to the big Victorian public library opened in Barking Road in 1894 where the legendary philanthropist John Passmore Edwards had donated its first thousand books. Because of Katy I was introduced to a world of reading far wider than anything I had discovered at school.

After her teenage working years, however, my aunt had settled down at home with her husband, Jack Palmer and a daughter Marion, three years older than me. Like my other four aunts, they had all somehow survived the bombs of World War Two. But unlike Katy, the Blitz and what followed had left its damaging aftermath on her husband.

Pipe-smoking uncle Jack was one of the quietest men I would ever meet. He spent a lot of time in his garden and a conducted tour, compulsory on every visit, was the best way for me to get him to talk and to know him a little. But as I was already interested in gardening this was no problem. Jack only grew dahlias — nothing else was allowed — and every bloom was at least four feet tall with massive heads adorned with enormous petals. While he puffed away, my uncle would break his silence to tell me about each of them; how they were planted, how he tended them and then stored the tubers in winter in his shed. They had been helped along with horse manure dug into his garden's soil, and Marion would laugh about his industrious solo trips with bucket and shovel whenever the clip-clop of horses' hooves was heard as they pulled a milkman's wagon or baker's dray along Star Lane. Every year Jack entered his luxurious blooms in a local flower show and regularly won top prizes. On the night before the show, each dahlia head on its stem would be lovingly encased in a paper bag to make sure that overnight rain could do no harm and so ensure his victory. But for Jack this simple gardening was more than a hobby; it was therapy. The unflagging bombing raids on Canning Town had shocked him into permanent post-traumatic stress syndrome and gardening, as well as the comforting level presence of his wife, was necessary to keep him calm.

Cousin Marion was big and no real beauty after she was grown. But — like her mother again — she had been clever at school, loved books and reading and was happy to read to me too; *Black Beauty* by Anna Sewell, *Anne of Green Gables* by Lucy Maud Montgomery with *Rupert Bear*, and *Noddy and Big Ears* for light relief. So at three years old I'd watch the words as she read, and soon began to recognise some of the shorter ones; a kick-start for reading when I began school. Later on, she took me to Barking Road library too, introducing me to Hans Christian Anderson and his tales.

In 1952, we went to see the movie too, starring Danny Kaye. At the same time, Marion had joined a youth group that was producing an on stage production of a musical at Green Gate's Baptist Church and Aunt Katy and I would go along to watch her daughter at rehearsals. With her I also learned *The Ugly Duckling*; one of the show's biggest and most charming songs by Frank Loesser who wrote the whole score including *Wonderful Copenhagen* and *The King's New Clothes*; two more huge hits for Kaye. Both of these turned up regularly on the BBC's *Children's Favourites* show which I listened to most weeks and which was presented, from 1954, by 'Uncle Mac' the broadcasting *nom-de-plume* of Derek McCulloch OBE. 'Uncle Mac' also took the part of *Larry the Lamb* in the BBC *Children's Hour* programme called *Toytown* and wrote the book called *A Child's Pilgrim's Progress*. So it was hard to believe the rumours later widely circulated — that our favourite radio relation of the time heartily disliked children of all ages.

When Marion's show was staged, we went to see it, and I was proud to see her, confident and word-perfect. This was something of a surprise: my cousin had a solitary streak but was happy to include me in her company. I would stay with Katy and her daughter during school holidays and on many mornings as a special treat my aunt would leave the house at daybreak to buy fresh rolls from a nearby local baker as soon as they opened their doors. Later Marion and I would explore Canning Town, stopping where anything interested us and going to the movies too, especially if they were in colour; rarer back then. My young friend could remember the words to a song from a film that we had only just seen, and I could sing along with her. We were a happy scruffy young duo.

Cousin Marion and me

A visit to Aunt Katy's was different from any of my other aunts. As overweight, slow in movement and speech as she was, she made me feel wanted and special: something that never happened to me at home now.

CHAPTER EIGHT

Back at 165 Kingston Road things were ever more difficult for my brother and I. Faithful unfailing Aunt Jessie had come in, as usual, to try and make friends and keep the peace with her new sister-in-law but it was to no avail; the two women would remain worlds apart. School friends invited to our house would be greeted by our stepmother with a turned head and resigned lift of her eyebrows. So we would stand and talk outside our front door.

In any case, our house by this time was far from the neat and tidy home that Louie had created; washing was piled up on the floor and plates were sometimes less than clean. Rose would regularly cook offal for supper — the unwanted entrails and organs of animals which came cheap at the butcher's — and her meals often smelt as bad as their ingredients. For breakfast, there would be cornflakes at best, though brother Jimmy, now well into his teens and in need of something more substantial, would tackle three pieces of shredded wheat. But Rose would never bother to heat the milk which made for difficult eating. And as her young son never seemed to eat anything much at all we were expected to do the same. Aunt Jessie once again came to the rescue by cooking bread pudding, and as Jimmy passed by in the street she would run out and press a big slice wrapped in grease-proof paper into his hands to keep him going.

But a lot of the time my brother was still hungry and regularly coming to blows with his once-loving father. So he was off and out first thing in the morning and soon I was cooking my own breakfast; more boiled eggs from our backyard chickens. Most things were rationed after the war in any case and the only thing that didn't seem to be was fish. But we never had home-cooked fish at home; fish and chips in newspaper from the shop were the best that our fast-fix stepmother could be bothered with.

By now though Salvation Army meetings were another reason to stay away from home at weekends. Back then with very few cars around most people still walked along Kingston Road. And one Sunday, before Rose had come along, a local redhead, Gertie, had knocked at the door and asked if I'd like to come to Sunday school. Why not? So with two more children every Sunday afternoon, we caught the bus to Barking, then walked along beside the railway track until we got to Ripple Road and the Army Citadel and climbed the stairs. The Citadel was a proper hall, purpose-built for the Army and complete with a band of young musicians in full uniform; the first time I'd ever seen real instruments played. Most of the officers wore uniforms too and the main idea seemed to keep our junior congregation amused while the grown-ups attended to the serious business of worship downstairs. There were only a couple of short prayers but right away we were asked to 'sign the pledge' forsaking alcohol forever, and I happily signed away along with my young companions. When I got back home afterwards my father asked if I'd had fun and what had I done?

"It was very good," I said, looking up at him, "and I signed the pledge!" My father roared with laughter.

I carried on going to Gertie's meetings for a couple of years, and after Rose arrived they were a big relief from new troubles at home. But I was older now, with my own interests and there was school and homework to be done. Brother Jimmy was seldom home to keep me company; he was out and about wheeling and dealing with his teenage friends and I was still too young to join them. So rather than go home I'd take my homework to the nearby library or stay in my bedroom if Graham wasn't there to read and read and read. But now school holidays rather than things to look forward to were miserable long-term sentences. And it was Aunt Nell — the eldest of the sisters and far away in Dunstable — who would take care of the problem come Summertime, the longest school holiday of all.

CHAPTER NINE

Aunt Nell

When I first stayed with Nell, she already had three grown-up children; Eddie the eldest, Donald, and Nell junior, always called 'Nen' to make things easy. Very confident, outspoken and the nearest thing to a real cockney of all her six sisters, Nell was the leader of their pack.

Her first husband in Canning Town had been Ted Ferguson. Like my father, Ted, had been employed at Beckton Gas Works, but it was Beckton which had put an end to him. The company ran a huge internal network of O-gauge tracks to carry coal and industrial machinery and one day in 1937 Ted was pinned under a moving train. It had ridden over him, his legs had been amputated, gangrene had set in amid the foul industrial airs around him, and he died. When Louie, pregnant with Jimmy heard the news she clapped the back of her neck in horror, giving her soon-to-be-born son a birthmark on the back of his own neck for life.

Very shortly after Nell met her second husband Mick Badcock; a name which prompted discreet giggles among her sisters. Mick was a greengrocer and he and his new wife and family set up home in Silvertown, North Woolwich, a few yards from London Docks. But from the start of World War Two Silvertown was a prime target for German bombs and on one occasion a ring of fire actually forced all the Woolwich ferries to mount a Dunkirk-style evacuation of every one of its inhabitants. The torrent of bombs levelling much of the landscape around them after 1940 was terrifying. And so, rather than waiting to be killed, Mick had loaded his horse and cart with his family and their possessions and all five had set out like gipsies on the road for Bedfordshire, over fifty miles away. It would have taken more than three days to get there with food and lodgings to find, and their horse to feed and rest. But somehow at last they ended up in Dunstable, found a house, settled in and never went back to east London again.

Jimmy had already been evacuated to Dunstable with Nell when he was five years old and I was glad to follow him on, almost ten years later, during school holidays. Nearby were the Downs on the edge of the Chiltern Hills, the highest point in Eastern England and one of the most famous beauty spots in Britain. I could watch gliders rise into the skies from the foot of the hills, fly a kite or gaze at historic barrows, the burial mounds of ancient kings. And when my adventures were over I could come back to Nell, the life of any party.

My aunt loved cheerful music and this was the era of such singers as the great Doris Day, Eve Boswell and Alma Cogan. Alma (known then as 'the girl with the laugh in her voice' and a good friend of the Beatles in their early days), was one of Nell's favourite singers, so walking down the street she was liable to launch into *If I had a Golden Umbrella* one of Cogan's biggest hits.

She knew I liked music too and if she heard me humming a tune would ask, 'what's that you're singing?' She would also say, 'come on now: sing me a song!' but at that point my mind would go blank. The same thing happens to me now — and to most people I think — if you say, 'tell me a joke!'. Daughter Nen was exactly like her mother; outgoing and ready to sing Al Jolson hits; *Mammie, Rosie* and *Toot Toot Tootsie* at any get-together. In fact, several of the sisters liked Jolson who styled himself: 'the world's greatest entertainer' and even Aunt Katy's Jack Russell terrier was called 'Tootsie'. They would have seen Jolson in the world's first talkie, *The Jazz Singer* in 1927.

When I first visited Nell, she was working at Dunstable Hospital as what, back then, was called a 'prep-cook'. This was long before frozen foods, so Nell worked with a big team of women colleagues to get vegetables ready for the patients' meals next day. Her speciality was potatoes and I would watch her hand-peeling hundreds of them, then throwing them into a zinc bath full of water with a big lump of coal in it. I didn't understand why but Nell explained that the carbon in the coal kept the potatoes 'sweet' for cooking the next day. All around her other women were happily shelling peas, washing lettuces, stripping carrots and any number of other vegetables and Nell would make sure that they made a great fuss of the little girl who was their guest.

"Have you come to see your Aunty Nell again?" was the question as they gathered around me with smiles, hugs and a kiss or two. Then Nell would lead us all in a singsong and there was no need to turn on the wireless for 'Music While You Work'; the BBC's programme, broadcast morning and afternoon, to encourage factory workers to stay cheerful. Nell and her ladies could raise the hospital roof all on their own.

Some of her relations were nice people too. George O'Shine her son-in-law who had married Nen had a twinkle in his eye and could make me laugh any time at all. Dark-haired Nen was beautiful and I thought she was as glamorous as a movie star. But like her mother, she did something else important to help me as I was beginning to grow up. She understood how to make women look good, was clever at make-up and keen to show me how to look after my hair; something I had never thought about before. With Nen I learned how to shampoo my hair, then dry it gently, not just give it a short sharp rub with a towel. This was early training in how to make myself look prettier, as well as some basic grounding in hairdressing; my profession for a while later on.

Rather than staying in beautiful Dunstable however, Nen and George decided to move back to rough old Silvertown later on. Why I have no idea but perhaps Nen had met George there when they were children. So my father would pay a call to see George and the two of them would find the nearest pub to catch up. He would bring me with him to see Nen too, and on the way I would stare in wonder at the massive ships as our bus rumbled through the docks, crossing their bascule bridges which, in a non-stop ballet, raised and lowered to let vessels through, and also, less obligingly, held up traffic at every corner. All of this grim blackened landscape, including Beckton Gas Works (now a housing estate optimistically renamed 'Beckton Alps'), has disappeared forever now under the miraculous transformation called 'Docklands', with its fairyland developments traversed by the Docklands Light Railway. But back then, when we alighted from the bus amid the slums, there was a fifty-foot high wall at the end of Nen's shabby street separating the road from the dock. And above the wall would tower a docked ship dwarfing the houses just a few yards away; an extraordinary meeting of sea and land.

Nell's son Eddie and his wife Pam had a son named Stephen. When I first visited their family Stephen was three years younger than me and the four of us would walk on the Downs with their big black Great Dane. The dog was docile and friendly but one day I was walking alone with Stephen and tickling him and my young charge was laughing and asking for more. The dog must have misunderstood his laughing for crying, and as I raised my hand to tickle again, he came forward and gently caught hold of my arm to stop me. He didn't let go, so I asked Stephen to get up and kiss me to show that nothing was wrong. Stephen did, and the big dog let go of my arm straight away. His mouth was so soft that he had left no mark on my arm at all. But it did make me realise that an animal could misunderstand a situation and react accordingly.

Eddie and his family lived in a 'prefab' nearby to his mother. Prefabs — really a prefabricated cabin using pre-assembled factory parts — are forgotten about now. But after the Second World War, they were wonderful inventions; ready for people who had lost their houses in bombing raids to move into straight away. Made of precast concrete panels reinforced with steel they were easy to put together and no specialist builder was needed to do the job. From the outside, they looked small and ordinary but inside they were quite spacious, with a garden and shed; you could move in right away and the only thing you needed to buy was a bed. There were wardrobes, only made of metal but wardrobes nevertheless; proper hot water systems and a bath and fully fitted kitchen units too. Later on, when they began to be demolished in favour of council houses, asbestos was discovered and there were some fatal results. But in 2021, clear of asbestos, there are still a few prefabs in existence and lived in too, and they fetch collector prices.

Aunt Nell, the nearest thing to 'the loud one' of her sisters, lived long enough to see Jimmy's children grow up and to mother them too, teaching them to sing the songs she loved. The Matriarch of the sisters she's gone now but her songs and her memories stay.

CHAPTER TEN

By now I was a pupil at Cleveland Road Junior School in Ilford, which had opened back in the 1890s. A big impressive building, it was the second in a series of School Board commissions for local architect C.J. Dawson. But for a little girl of eight Cleveland looked formidable and forbidding. Its classrooms had high ceilings and windows; so tall that the teacher would have to use a long pole with a hook at the end to open or shut them. For most of my school years, I was happy, but do remember that the school dinners were awful. We only managed to eat them as food at home, under Rose's regime, was in such short supply.

In the corner of the playground there was a huge heap of coal to stoke the central heating and my brother Jimmy remembered that somehow, on the tarmac playground, he and a group of boys had managed to set up a game of cricket. How they put the stumps in I can't imagine. But Jimmy's first six to the imaginary boundary had gone straight through a classroom window putting a premature end to the game.

Cleveland had its celebrations, however. By Christmas 1953 the newly crowned Queen Elizabeth II and Duke of Edinburgh were at the start of a tour of the

Commonwealth on the royal yacht Britannia. By then we had all watched her Coronation on television six months beforehand on June 2nd; a very big day indeed. Many families in Britain bought their first-ever television set to watch the ceremony with its spectacular golden coach (reduced to a black and white screen), but for some households, the cost was too high. We couldn't afford one either, but opposite us in Kingston Road lived the Halls family who (at least for Ilford), were what today would be called 'upwardly mobile'. Their daughter, Lesley, three years younger than me, had become a friend, and from time to time, I was invited in to have tea with her; a very proper affair. So when the coronation came along it was Mr and Mrs Hall who had the first television in the street and invited all the neighbourhood children in to watch the ceremony. Because I was friends with Lesley, I was high on the list of invitations, but as I remember most of the other junior viewers fell by the wayside. Only I made it through to the very end.

After the Coronation it was time for our new Queen to travel to every country in the Commonwealth, still a thriving international community. In her Christmas day broadcast which we all listened to at Kingston Road, she had said: *my husband and I left London a month ago, but we have already paid short visits to Bermuda, Jamaica, Fiji and Tonga, and have passed through Panama. I should like to thank all our hosts very warmly for the kindness of their welcome and the great pleasure of our stay. In a short time, we shall be visiting Australia and later Ceylon and before we end this great journey we shall catch a glimpse of other places in Asia, Africa and the Mediterranean.*

So now it was time for Cleveland Road School to play its part and it was decided that we should all dress up for 'Commonwealth Day' (later called Empire Day), on the second Monday in March. Nobody could help me back at home but we went ahead at school and with five other pupils, complete with grass skirts, I was chosen to be a New Zealand Māori. For Ilford, this was quite a complicated business. First of all, raffia (the nearest thing to grass we could find), had to be ordered for the skirts and when it arrived the teacher had to show us how to loop it around our waists. Then we found coloured shirts to go on top with raffia garlands around our necks and headpieces to top off our costumes. On the day we all appeared in our huge playground and it made for a colourful show. There were Africans, Asians, Caribbeans, Australians, Arabs and Indians and we had to find a dance to do as well. Then we were taken back into school and shown where our countries were on the map and that we were just what our new Queen had said: part of a great international community.

Back in Addington Road, where our hosts were Mary and her husband, Jim, we also had a street party to celebrate the Coronation. There were long trestle tables with lots of food and drink and all the children were dressed up in costumes. Mine, for some reason, was the Queen of Hearts complete with a tray of tarts which Mary baked for me.

Me, fully tarted up

My aunt loved knitting, always had patterns and her needles to hand, and one of her specialities was sweaters. To these bright garments, she regularly added a decorative parrot on their shoulders and on one occasion for me a pair of the brightly coloured birds; I did my best to look pleased. On another occasion, she fitted me out with a warm Harris Tweed winter coat in brown and green. Then she completed the new outfit with a hat, gloves and scarf all in bright yellow and all of which arrived on the same day that we had a school day out in Autumn to visit High Beach, a tiny village in the heart of Epping Forest. This was a field trip to look for everything from autumn leaves, mushrooms and toadstools (luckily our teacher told us the difference), to acorns and berries that were left over from Summer. Unusually I was late for school that day (probably because I was busy trying on Mary's new ensemble), and when I finally arrived in the classroom got a black look from our teacher and looks of astonishment from the pupils around me. Out of my school uniform for once, in my bright yellow rig, I was definitely a fashion plate for the day.

But the visit to High Beach was marvellous. It was the first time I'd ever been to a real forest with the wonderful leafy smell of the 'season of mists and mellow fruitfulness' that Keats wrote about in his *Ode to Autumn*.

Sweaters aside, however, Aunt Mary was another of the sisters to play a big part in my early years. She thought it was time for me to get some fun out of life.

CHAPTER ELEVEN

Aunt Mary Read

It had all begun when my mother was becoming more and more ill and I'd been regularly sent over to stay for the weekend with Mary and Jim in Canning Town. It was explained to me that 'mother needs to take a rest' again and I was happy to go along with the idea as Mary was great fun. On earlier visits to Addington Road, she and my mother had talked non-stop. There was always laughter and secret giggles too, and when we left, we would talk about how Mary had made us feel good.

She was Louie's younger sister by three years; outgoing, fun and fair of face with a beautiful complexion, and regular visits to the hairdresser stopped her light blonde hair from turning grey. But after Louie died Mary went into shock and her hair began to fall out. My aunt didn't waste time when problems arose, so promptly she booked into the Poplar hospital for infra-red treatment and I would watch as we came back home to see if her hair would miraculously grow back on the spot. My fervent wishes couldn't be granted of course, but Mary's hair grew back gradually over a year or two and she was happy again.

By this time, I was seven years old and continuing to grow up fast and another problem that Mary had to deal with, was how to keep me looking smart. If I needed a new pair of shoes she would say, "you should ask Dad." But if James couldn't, or wouldn't step in, it was my aunt who did instead. This kind of generosity extended to my junior wardrobe too. Unlike my mother, she was no seamstress but found a recommendation to a Mrs Mills in East Ham, and together we went to pay her a visit.

I couldn't believe this wonderful elderly lady's workroom which, rather than a tidy selection of sorted fabrics looked as if it had been ransacked, leaving a rainbow cornucopia of brightly coloured materials flung everywhere, and reels of coloured cottons dotted haphazardly in any available space as well as all over the floor. It was a mesmerising sight; Mrs. Mills measured me up, we agreed on a green check material, and after we came away I couldn't stop asking Mary how my new dressmaker could possibly know where anything at all was, apart – presumably – from her sewing machine? But a fortnight later, there was the mock-up of my new dress to be pinned on for a few prickly final adjustments before the final creation was ready, two more weeks later. And so, for the next eight or more years my generous Aunt would carry on taking me back to Mrs. Mills for all my clothes, until I was fifteen and old enough to find a Saturday job in a shoe-shop to buy dresses of my own. This was an expensive business and no doubt it was fortunate that my aunt was a working woman at Standard Telephones in Silvertown

There was always something going on at her house once work was over and Mary was determined that I should enjoy life whatever was going on back in Ilford. So she would plan treats for me and as soon as one was over she was on her way to the next. For several years these included the spectacular Christmas ice shows at London's Empress Hall. I loved them for the skating as well as the music and songs. One, when I was seven in 1951, was *London Melody*, starring the legendary British comedian Norman Wisdom and the superb Olympic figure-skater Belita (really Maria Belita Jepson-Turner), who appeared in movies for Monogram Pictures. Another in 1954 was

White Horse Inn on Ice starring Max Wall. Max was funny enough on foot, but on skates, he was more hilarious still.

Another of Mary's favourite trips was shopping in London's Oxford Street. We'd travel upstairs on the number twenty-five bus and watch everything happening along the way. There were still bomb sites all around us and it intrigued me to see how wild flowers and plants were so quickly taking over the bare ground; nature's benign restorative to damage and tragedy.

One day when I was eight years old, she told me that they were finally going to stop running trams in South Woolwich. 'Operation Tramaway', the replacement of the tram service by double-decker buses, was announced in July 1950 by Lord Latham of the London Transport Executive. London's final first-generation trams were due to make just one more run in the early hours of 6 July 1952 before they would disappear from London for half a century more. And we were there on the day. Mary had many likes but she loved the trams and decided we should take one last trip around south-east London.

So we set out early from Canning Town on one of the new double-decker buses and travelled to North Woolwich where we boarded the ferry with the ship's enormous engine pumping its gigantic pistons up and down; beautiful and spotlessly clean. Then at South Woolwich, we made the short walk to the stop. I had never been on a tram before, was looking forward to the ride like my aunt and it was plain that we weren't the only ones. The whole week beforehand every one of the old vehicles had carried a banner so there was a packed queue of passengers just as excited as us and quite a bustle to get on board. But Mary and I managed to stay together and sit side by side, while I sat in the window seat listening to her running travelogue on sights to see. There was excitement all around us; our conductor was in high spirits as he punched tickets proclaiming, 'Last Tram Week' and the whole journey lasted for an extra three hours because of thousands of cyclists riding along with us and thousands more cheering Londoners surrounding the tracks from Woolwich to New Cross. I saw a tear or two in my aunt's eyes as we rolled along the old rails one last time.

The party to say goodbye to London trams went on into the small hours at New Cross Depot; long after Mary and I had come home with our memories. For the last journey of all the driver was John Cliff, then deputy

Chairman of London Transport, who had begun his career years before driving trams along the route he had now agreed to close.

A year or two before, Mary told me about a new festival on the south bank of the River Thames. This was to be the now legendary 'Festival of Britain'; the first fantastic statement of Britain's return to greatness after the war. It was also a clever political move to boost public *morale* by Clement Attlee's post-war labour government which was now losing ground. So, Attlee laid the foundation stone in 1949; many of the old warehouses along the Thames were quickly demolished to make way for new buildings on the site, and by May 1950 everything was ready to go.

Just one year later, hundreds of thousands of people including Mary, husband Jim and I flocked to the South Bank to wander around the 'Dome of Discovery', gaze at the fifty-foot 'Skylon' (the joke was: 'it has no visible means of support!') and the brand-new 'Royal Festival Hall' where orchestras were conducted by Sirs Adrian Boult and Malcolm Sargent, known as 'Flash' whose recording of the *Hallelujah Chorus* from Handel's *Messiah* was famous (or possibly the opposite!) as the fastest thing on record!

The buildings were quite literally like a new world to me. They were clean, brightly coloured and — wonder of wonders — completely free from the sooty blackness which was so much a part of my family's life in the East End. I didn't much care for the avant-garde angularity of some of them but no doubt: this was a new world. After the exhibitions there was more to come; pleasure gardens had appeared which would later become 'Battersea Fun Fair', with its legendary 'Big Dipper' which only closed in the late 1970s. A miniature railway designed by Rowland Emmett ran for 500 yards along the south of the gardens with a station near the entrance called 'Far Tottering'; a name we loved. There was a restaurant with a terrace overlooking the river and facing Cheyne Walk on its north side. And the wet weather pavilion intrigued me too as it faced two ways — one stage facing inwards and the other for open-air presentations. There were huge murals by film set designer Ferdinand Bellan, something else I'd never seen before, and an amphitheatre seating 1250 people which was later turned into a circus. Everywhere was music and dancing; people were eating, drinking and having a good time. One of the best things I saw was the grandly-named 'Foaming Fountain' lake; bigger than any boating pool I'd ever seen. My uncle took me on the pool too; its boats had tiny engines, not oars, so I was allowed to take the wheel, and afterwards we had strawberry ice-cream too; another first for me and — just perhaps — the best part of an unforgettable day.

For four years Mary and Jim also took me on summer holidays to Eastchurch where we stayed in a caravan. There were fields all around and I could play for hours on the cliff heights, fly a kite or watch the birds below me in the sky. For one holiday Mary treated me to my first-ever pair of jeans which I loved and took with me. But ever the tomboy I then spent happy hours sliding up and down the cliffs and when I arrived back at the caravan for tea, Mary spotted the split in my rear end in mock dismay. "You've been arsed out!" she said — an expression I'd never heard my demure aunts use before — and Mary had to patch up my beautiful new jeans. I was mortified while my aunt got busy with her industrious needle and thread.

But Mary was not just fun but domestically ambitious too. She always wanted the newest kitchen appliance and was the first of the sisters to own a top-loader washing machine, a Bendix, and very modern for its day. Next came a fridge, then a modern cooker, a pressure cooker for good luck and after that a water heater for the kitchen. One more luxury was an electric toaster — no sitting in front of the fire with a long toasting fork waiting for just the right moment when the bread turned brown, or the wrong one when it caught fire. And there was something else about Mary; she seemed to be able to find food which you couldn't find anywhere else. After all those years Canning Town's Rathbone Street market was still there and my taste buds were set alive.

The excitement never seemed to stop and neither did the adventures. Mary loved staying up to date, and for several years took me to the 'Ideal Home Exhibition' at Olympia, North London. It would be a long day, but Mary made sure that we had food and drink to keep our energy levels up while we marvelled at all the domestic miracles of the 1950s. Many of the visiting couples had married after the war and looked enviously at shiny new domestic innovations: fully fitted kitchens and bathrooms, food mixers, coffee makers, cookers, refrigerators, radios and televisions.

In 1957, long before womens' liberation, the average British wife still spent an average of seventy hours a week on housework. So, over the years, Mary was determined to make her modest terraced house the smartest in the street. Central heating (quite rare then), an indoor bathroom, and carpets and curtains with matching blinds all appeared at maximum speed, along with every other new luxury that came along year by year. So where did all this extra money come from? My uncle was a betting man and there were whisperings between the sisters that Jim and Mary had had a win on the pools too. But we never really knew.

Her front room also had a state of the art radiogram, and a big selection of 78s and vinyl LPs which I was allowed to play at weekends; quite a privilege for a six year old. So I heard some of Mary's favourites — Max Bygraves, Teresa Brewer, the Big Ben Banjo Band — and also the scores and songs from classic musicals including *South Pacific* and *Oklahoma* which I could quickly learn to sing for myself, lyrics and all. Mary bought lots of new records too including Frank Sinatra, and when she found out that I liked Frank too began buying more, so I couldn't wait to find out what she'd brought home from the record shop. Then there were the big bands — Benny Goodman and Glenn Miller — which I discovered almost as soon as I could read their names on the labels. This had a lot to do with my lifelong love of jazz and my marriages later to two jazz musicians: first clarinettist, Dave Claridge, and later my present husband, trumpet-cornetist, Digby Fairweather.

CHAPTER TWELVE

But now I was coming up for eleven years old, and my first secondary school. Mount School for Girls in Uphall Road Ilford was only a mile away from home; a basic seat of learning which assumed that its pupils would work for a while in an office, then get married and have a family. So we were taught basic domestic skills; cooking, cleaning, sewing, washing and ironing, along with simple maths, English, music (surprisingly!), and geography. Not very exciting, but classical music was played before assembly, so I made a point of arriving early.

But now my womanly curves were beginning to appear prompting some awkward moments. Every year we would have a medical at school, stripped down to our panties for the purpose, and very soon I came to grief as, well ahead of my classmates, it was clear that I was developing breasts and nipples. So next year I asked to keep my vest on. But once again it was Aunt Mary who went into action right away as soon as I took my coat off. "You need a bra now," she said and marched me smartly to the nearest store the next day to get my newly formed curves controlled.

At Mount School all our teachers were single women — and therefore called 'Miss' — and rumour had it that if they married, they would have to leave work as nurses in hospitals were required to do. Our maths teacher was Miss Peake but contrary to her name, she was tiny and had to stand on a box to reach her blackboard at all. Unfortunately, she also had two sets of spectacles with identical frames but different lenses. So, she would climb onto the box only to find she had the wrong ones on to see her blackboard; come down again to change them, and then be unable to see to get back up on her box.

But despite her eccentricities (and her pupils' suppressed giggles), Miss Peake was liked by all her young charges. She was a new-age philanthropist as well, and one day in 1955 asked us to give whatever we could to send to war-torn children caught in the Algerian War of Independence. This was decades before such contributions to international troubles were daily requests on television, and Miss Peake agreed to double our contributions which we were happy to give, and which she doubled accordingly.

One day she asked me to stay behind after class. I wondered what I'd done wrong but my teacher told me about the thirteen-plus examination, designed for pupils who had narrowly missed grammar school. She said that I should be thinking about taking the exam and offered to take on additional teaching for me after school. There would be extra homework too, but Miss Peake would help me to do it and there would be no charge. While I didn't recognize the magnanimity of my teacher's offer at the time I knew that I wanted to take advantage of it very much indeed.

Back at 165 Kingston Road no one was much interested in my news so instead, I told Aunt Mary that weekend. And it was Mary who told me right away that I must, at all costs, take Miss Peake's advice, and the exam too. This was a challenge, but in the weeks to come my teacher showed me previous exam papers, asked me to answer their questions and marked them afterwards. If I'd failed something or answered a question wrongly she would put me right on the facts and also tell me about standard subjects that often came up in new exam papers. It would be a good idea to research these, she said, and found time to help me with my maths too; all work well beyond the call of her duty.

In short, marvellous Miss Peake went the extra mile for me and with her practical and entirely unpaid help — along with my aunt's unfailing encouragement — I passed the thirteen-plus exam and won my place at Beal Grammar School for Girls in Ley Street Ilford. A great teacher can take you a long way in life and tiny Miss Peake had done exactly that. I hope I found time to thank her.

When I started at Beal, I had to wear a school uniform for the first time. People sometimes argue against uniforms for school. But for me, they were a happy leveller as some of my new school colleagues came from families with plenty of money (and clothes) and trying to search for a clean new dress every day back at shabby Kingston Road had been a chore at least, and sometimes impossible. So at Beal, we dressed alike and I loved the uniforms too. In summer we wore a brown and white gingham dress, a brown blazer with school badge and a straw hat. In winter we changed to a brown pinafore dress, cream shirt, brown and gold striped tie and blazer topped with a brown mackintosh and beret with our badge again. Then there was the kit for gym; a cream tee-shirt, brown panties and *culotte* shorts with brown plimsolls, long before trainers came in. All in all, an expensive business and no doubt my father and stepmother felt the financial strain. Perhaps one or more of my aunts chipped in too. But somehow, I got my uniforms.

For the first two years, I had to work very hard indeed to catch up with my fellow students. There were twenty latecomers like me — all thirteen-plus graduates — and as soon as we arrived we were sent for by our headmistress Miss Coleman. After a brief efficient greeting, she told us that we were lucky to be in the school, but that we were two years behind everyone and would have to do a lot of work to catch up. The school, Miss Coleman said, had a high record of exam results with many pupils going straight on to college and later to university. So, she expected us to fit in with their schedule without special treatment and the only thing that we would not expect to study was Latin, still very much on the syllabus at the time. For a substitute, an alternative for university entrance, we would take Greek literature in translation. I was a long way from Kingston Road now!

I soon realised that my broad East London accent wouldn't and didn't fit in with my classmates, so I quickly set about some personal voice training; smoothing out vowel sounds, noting the business of glottal-stops for consonants and much else. My English teacher was a great help with this. She was particular about grammar and pronunciation but would never single a pupil out, preferring to pick up mistakes around the class as they occurred: saving added embarrassment about what was left of my cockney accent and grammatical gaffs. This was more important then; the 1950s were still the era of what was once called 'Received English', the accent of Oxford, Cambridge and of course the BBC, long before the Beatles made regional accents fully acceptable. So, as my voice improved, it became easier for me to fit in on equal terms with the rest of the girls. In the main they came from middle-class families; their fathers were businessmen and I was being invited into homes that were nothing like the untidy, unhappy shambles that was my own. Now I was a new-age teenager; developing confidence and ideas of my own, and my world was opening up.

At Beal most of the girls had bicycles too. When I was ten, I'd already acquired my first full-size bike; an elderly BSA with only three gears and sit-up-and-beg handlebars. But my resourceful brother had found a screwdriver and made the best of things by turning them upside down to give my heavy machine the beginnings of a sporty drop-handlebar look. So, after I arrived at Beal, four friends — Linda, Margaret, Fran and Gillian — and I decided to join the South East Essex Cycling Club. This was a serious affair. The organizer was Adrian; he would plan our trips and timetable their dates over the weekend.

There was training in the evenings too. We would meet at a set point; usually Gallows Corner Romford, as our riders came from all over east London; Chigwell, Leytonstone, Wanstead, Upminster and further afield. We'd assemble at seven p.m. usually in a pub car park, and cycle down the A127 to the Halfway House, a distance of around seven miles. In those days the road had a cycle track at its side, but it was years old so there were ruts, bumps and potholes to contend with, and soon we'd take to the main road. Once arrived at the Halfway House there was a roundabout (it's long gone now), and there we would make for home.

Then at weekends, we would go on time trials. I'd never heard of these before but they were exactly that; a personal trial to see how quickly you could get around a course — say twenty miles — within a set time. We'd get ready for them by cycling up to a tiny Essex village (unfortunately called 'Ugley') on Saturday evenings and stay in a broken-down hut. This was divided into two areas — boys at one end, girls at the other — separated by nothing more than a hanging blanket suspended across the room. There was a basic toilet outside (nothing new there), and we'd sleep in sleeping bags or on a mattress or whatever else we could find.

The trials started early in the morning at seven a.m. Adrian had a team of four stewards all with stopwatches placed around the course, and one at the finishing line. 'Ready, steady, go!' came the command and off we went. Girls would always go first; each girl individually followed by girl number two, two minutes later, until we were all under way. Then the same thing would happen with the boys. The course would be circular, around twenty miles in all, and the more experienced riders could make the circuit five times. The first time I did it I made two circuits, then three, then four and finally five — the full hundred miles — over about a year.

The fun, first of all, was to catch up with the first girl ahead of you, then overtake her. Best of all was to start catching up with some of the boys. They were distinctly reluctant to let me do it so they'd go faster until they couldn't find any more speed and past them, I would go. One up to the girls!

I was still riding my rusty old BSA complete with its homemade drop handlebars, but it was quick-eyed Aunt Mary who once again turned up trumps. My friends had come to her home in Addington Road to meet me and she had noticed that everybody else in the team had a far better bike than me. So somewhere she found a lightweight second-hand cycle; well looked after in sporty black and yellow. This was not only an unexpected bonus but I found the hard slog on my old heavy machine had toughened me up, and on my new light bike it felt as if I was riding the wind. So, I started to think about much longer trips with my cycling team. And it would turn out that one plan, in particular, would bring about the biggest, most violent and traumatic crisis back in my troubled home in Kingston Road.

But that was later and meantime I carried on working hard. There was still lots of homework to do; sometimes at home (if I kept out of the way); sometimes at school if there was a free period in a spare classroom or sometimes in the big Ilford library. But by the age of fifteen, I'd caught up with my studies and was also starting to get out on my own, dancing in Ilford jazz clubs with a new school friend Fran. But the friendship was short; Fran fell in love with Cliff Richard at first hearing and went to see a live concert with Cliff and the Shadows, after which — like the whole of the UK in years to come — she fell in love with Sir Cliff Richard forever. So, I was without a jazz friend but still in love with the music, so I went on my own, just to dance. I was also starting to think about boyfriends.

But in the meantime, every week, I was still cycling back to Canning Town to see my aunts — including the last two of the seven sisters. And they were Ivy and Liddie.

CHAPTER THIRTEEN

Ivy and John

Ivy was the youngest of the seven sisters and when I was first aware of her, I was still only three years old. By then she had met John Smith and marriage was on the way. She had met her man while he was working on London Docks but he had joined the army as a junior private and after the war was sent out to Malta where he found himself working in the docks again, this time in his army uniform.

Ivy worked at Gill Brothers, a tobacco and cigarette factory nearby to her home in Canning Town and as a result, both she and her husband turned into smokers for life. It's hardly surprising that I remember the two of them because on the day they married, 29th March 1947, it was not only my third birthday, but the afternoon of the Boat Race when Cambridge (my team in later years) won, and sadly for local football fans, West Ham lost to Coventry City, two goals to one. Quite a triple to be imprinted on my young mind! But what I certainly didn't know then was that for John and Ivy it was a cannily profitable date to set for marriage too; couples regularly did so before the end of March to redeem income tax before the start of the new financial year. So romance and finance were both in the air. Their wedding was a big family affair: all seven sisters and their husbands attended with children and friends. My grandmother was there too one year before she died, and this was certainly the last time all the family were photographed together.

Ivy and John set up a home in a ground floor flat at thirty-five Durham Road, Canning Town, where my grandmother still lived with cousin Nen and husband George next door. Before too long, John took a job as a crane-driver on the docks and gradually the couple saved enough to lay down a mortgage on a small house in nearby Gerald Road, a few doors away from Aunt Liddie. They moved in taking their prized wedding presents with them; one of them an electric toaster, very modern for its day I thought (in fact I was wrong; they had been around for almost fifty years), and a small refrigerator, the first one I had ever seen. Like her mother and mine Ivy also owned a new treadle sewing machine costing £17.50. But it needed an electric motor so John bought one which also cost £17.50; an expensive investment and over £1,300 in today's money.

Ivy was warm and friendly, enjoyed the company of my mother or Aunt Jessie on visits, and always smiled when she saw us at her front door. Sometimes, like Jessie, she would give me sweets too; a big treat as they were still on ration. But I did notice the smoking. This was an everyday thing for people back then but for some reason, I already felt that women shouldn't smoke at all, and perhaps it was the cigarettes that put an end to John much too early. But Ivy stayed at Gerald Road until, after a compulsory purchase order, the whole block of houses was demolished to make way for a single patch of green grass. By then she was a widow and was offered a nearby flat where she settled in for the rest of her days.

But although I loved my six aunts not all the visits were not quite so joyful.

Sometimes Aunt Jessie would take me to see her elder sister Elizabeth always known as 'Liddie'. Liddie had had two sons by her first husband John but soon after, however, she had married Billy Rose, a one-time bantamweight boxer who by now was a busker playing in local pubs to scratch a living. Early on our Christmas get-togethers had always been at Liddie's house too. But at Liddie's house, it didn't always feel like Christmas. Shorter and even more timid than Jessie she never seemed as happy as her sisters, seldom smiled and sometimes I would see tears in her eyes when we visited and the two of them said hello. Then they would find a private place to talk quietly; for now, it was plain, they didn't want me to hear what they were saying. Afterwards, they would come and find me — usually looking at a magazine or book — and then I was invited to join the conversation.

It was years later that I found out what the private talk had been about. Regularly Billy Rose had beaten up his wife and sometimes we could not visit as Liddie would have a black eye or a bruise on her cheek. Jessie and my aunts would know all about it, and we would be asked to stay away. Later, Billie tried it on her two sons too, and they floored their stepfather.

Liddie and Bill Rose

One thing I noticed was that when Jessie and Liddie got together their cockney side came out. Although they were born in London's East End, all seven sisters had always done their best to speak well most of the time. But when Liddie and Jessie were together they peppered their conversation with real cockney slang and I soon learned that 'a gamp' was an umbrella; 'a globe' a light bulb and other old words you never hear now.

Opposite her house was a derelict school, a victim of wartime bombing, which added a feeling of hopelessness, and Liddie's home was by no means spick and span with none of the up-to-date post-war innovations that Mary had acquired. An old cast iron kitchen range in her living room gave off a sooty smell and there were other out-of-date oddities in the house including a radio with an accumulator, rather like a prehistoric battery, which had to be earthed. As her small backyard was concrete this meant that an actual bucket of earth had to stand outside a back window into which the earth rod was pushed. Even the voltage in Canning Town was different back then. Generators were provided for electricity — probably the dockside power stations had been bombed — and the whole of the area was powered by just 210 volts. Any defunct light bulb (or globe), had to be taken to the nearby electricity company to be replaced free of charge.

Of all seven sisters, Liddie was the saddest. But for better or worse she stayed with Billy until the end of her days. And when she did smile her pretty face turned to sunshine.

CHAPTER FOURTEEN

Back at Beal Grammar School for Girls my first boyfriend was Arthur, a pupil at Beal's all-male branch for boys. This was a separate building but every so often our schools came together for sports days, and two of my friends and I met three boys: a neat arrangement. My girlfriends thought Arthur was the best looking, and one day he asked me to go to the pictures. But it was a silent affair; we met at the top of my road, walked wordlessly to the Regal cinema, saw the film and then went for an equally speech-free milkshake at the Black and White Milk Bar in Ilford Broadway. After that he walked me home, the silence as good as unbroken; there was no goodnight kiss and poor Arthur left me to get his bus home.

Probably I wasn't much help. Back in those days, I was used to talking to boys and girls alike about most things but it was my second husband, Digby Fairweather, a one-time sufferer, who explained to me what a debilitating handicap shyness can be for young men. Actor David Kossoff even produced a poem about them in his book of 'small prayers' called *Have you a minute, Lord?*.

What's the point of shyness?
Modesty yes, sense of proportion, yes.

Quietness, respect for others, yes.
But shyness?
Tongue-locked, brain-locked,
Turned-in, turned off,
Eye-lowered, head-lowered Hell?

Perhaps that was what poor Arthur was going through and maybe I could have helped him more but every conversational gambit I offered was returned with a monosyllable and I didn't understand why. Wherever you are Arthur I'm sorry.

Then there was Michael who I met at our table tennis club. He began walking me home and after two or three trips asked me to go to the pictures again; we sat in the back row and I wondered what might happen. Nothing did but on the way home, he was the first to want to feel my breasts now in full flower. I stopped him but he got his kiss and went home, no doubt with bigger things on his mind and possibly elsewhere too.

After that Michael asked me home for tea where I met his French mother. She was lovely and so was his father — I often liked my boyfriends' parents more than the boys — and in their big Austin car they took us out for motor trips. Sitting in the back Michael was clearly interested in my bosom again and tried to examine it more closely but I pushed him away; his mother and father could clearly see us in their rear mirror. After that, things stopped; Michael would like to have gone a lot further but I was worried and didn't know what to do. This was years before the pill and besides, where could we go? Michael wouldn't have been allowed in at 165 Kingston; none of my aunts, however much they loved me, would be ready to turn a blind eye, and there was no other refuge.

When I started at Beal one of the families I visited had a son called John. Once again they were nice people; interested in all the school's activities and even helped us with our homework. Then John joined our cycling club making us nine in all — Linda, Margaret, Fran and Gillian along with Peter, Frank and Ben. Gillian had a lot of trouble with two-wheel cycles so Ben who thought she was nice bought a tandem so she could ride behind him and they became boy and girlfriend. So did Peter and Linda and so, by degrees, did John and me.

By this time, our cycling trips were starting to take us a lot further; first into Suffolk and Norfolk, then to Devon and finally Scotland. Sometimes there were no youth hostels to be had so we would take tents. And one night John and I ended up in one of the tents together kissing and cuddling.

But then things went further. I was wearing baby-doll pyjamas and very gently together we took the panties off and eager erect John entered me for the first time. I had very little idea of what was happening but was ready for him and not, for the moment, worried about pregnancy; nevertheless an unforgivable sin in 1961 when the swinging sixties had yet to dawn. But before he ejaculated John withdrew just in time. From a devout catholic family, he knew that he couldn't use protection (most young people were too embarrassed to buy what we called

'French letters' in the chemist anyhow) and had probably practised the art of leaving the holy chamber before anything went wrong — quite a skill for a young man still in his teens. So, after it was quickly over, and though I hadn't reached any sort of climax, he was able to explain to me what had happened and why. This would be the first of several passionate meetings. I was fond of John and thought at the time I loved him. But once again, it was really his family that I loved more; to be part of a family again, after the hateful years at 165 Kingston, was probably just as important as the sex we were beginning to discover together. Gradually, John and I would see less of each other; a teenage romance which like many others would fade to a memory with time.

But in the meantime we had begun plans for our biggest cycling trip, this time to the western highlands of Scotland. This was ambitious, to say the least, and we would have to save for the rail journey to Glasgow; a major financial challenge for me even though we were going to take the cheapest overnight train, stopping at every station on the way. So I managed to find a Saturday job in 'Richard Shops'; the women's' fashion store in Ilford High Road and started to save for the trip straight away.

However, stepmother Rose made herself felt, and decided that the savings from my Saturday job should contribute to her household funds. She would be 'speaking to James' about it too. A few days later, and alone in the house, my once-loving father sided with his wife point-blank, despite my explanations that it was the only way I could save for the train fare and hostel payments for the trip to Scotland. By now though I was a teenager with a mind of my own and the argument between us got heated; an obdurate father and rebellious daughter fighting for supremacy for the first time.

Then without warning my father lost his temper and swung at me. He was still a swarthy fit man and his blow sent my head through the heavy glass panel of a nearby open door. For a moment I had no idea what had happened but within seconds realised that blood was falling down my face and all the way down my clothes. I was in shock but all I knew now was that I needed to get away from my father and my hateful stepmother, forever.

So along the road I ran to my Aunt Jessie at 251 Kingston and knocked frantically on her door. By now I was crying too; blood was everywhere and my aunt was speechless when she saw me. But she took me indoors; found a towel to wipe some of the blood away and did her best to calm me down. Shaking with shocked trauma, I was barely aware of what was happening; only that my stepmother had arrived to assure Jessie that she hadn't been present when the damage was done and also, of course, that she had had nothing to do with it. Then she made her exit, assuaged of guilt.

My aunt knew that a doctor was essential and took me to our surgery when it opened at six o' clock. We had to join other patients in the waiting room and by now I had a throbbing headache and only wanted to go to bed. But for some lucky reason brother Jimmy arrived, saw my plight and somehow persuaded everybody that I should jump the queue. The doctor patched me up and asked how the accident had happened? Jessie told him that I had 'taken a fall' looking directly at me to make sure that I understood her alibi; she feared a police arrival at the door of 165 Kingston Road.

After that I never ever wanted to go back home and if I was forced to do so, avoided my father and stepmother at all costs. I also began to make plans to leave home and visited my local Citizens' Advice Bureau, where I made an appointment to see a solicitor a week later. He told me that I couldn't be forced to come back home once I'd left. But meanwhile it was ever-faithful Aunt Jessie, who had told the whole story to sister Mary. Then Mary had gone to see my father and he had agreed that I could move in permanently with her. So now I knew I would never need to see my father again. But the livid scar was on my forehead for years after and this was the end of the road.

In the meantime I had plans for a nursing career but for now this was impossible: NHS regulations meant that I couldn't pursue my calling until I was eighteen. So, while my other friends were moving on to college, there was only one thing to do. I had to find a job.

CHAPTER FIFTEEN

Safely back with Mary and Jim I still had nine months before I could begin nursing. So I answered an advertisement for a post as trainee fashion buyer at London's biggest and most luxurious fashion store, Harrods of Knightsbridge. In London's Brompton Road Harrods had been a legend for a century and its clients over the years had included Oscar Wilde, Lillie Langtry, Ellen Terry, Charlie Chaplin, Noël Coward, Gertrude Lawrence, Laurence Olivier and Vivien Leigh, Sigmund Freud, A. A. Milne, and members of the Royal Family. If the Queen wanted to shop there Harrods would close its doors in the evening so that her Majesty could browse at leisure. And at Harrods you could buy anything at all. One department I remember in particular was the food hall on the ground floor. It was palatial and its fish hall alone consisted of a huge glossy tiled area which extended to the top of the store wall with a rainbow display of fish arranged on ice in patterns. Today the store has a 'fish bar' — rather less spectacular — but back then Harrods' fish hall was a wonderous sight.

I got the job and the week before I started work had a letter telling me how and where to arrive. This was in the next block to the main store; you went in on the ground floor to the clocking-in department and on the day a group of twenty of us were met by the first of our professional mentors. She led us on a mysterious journey through a huge subterranean landscape under the store, then into a lift and up again, this time to the training floor. There we were met by three tutors; all of them smart, beautifully dressed and made up, and well-spoken. I was glad that I had trained my own voice at Beal Grammar so that I wouldn't feel out of place. But I still had to watch myself as most of my fellow newcomers had homes in Surrey and ponies of their own to ride at the weekend. I simply couldn't allow myself to make a slip and reveal my roots as a one-time cockney girl from Canning Town. 'Best not do that' as Aunt Jessie had reminded me.

The training included basic information about how the mighty institution called 'Harrods' ran from day to day; an orientation tour around the whole building, and once we were assigned to a department, what our duties would be. The first requirement was to arrive on time to the minute. This was after clocking-in; on its own a fifteen-minute walk from our department. Then, we were told, we must always look much more than just presentable. We could wear black and white only, usually a black skirt, a white blouse and if necessary a black jacket too. So, we had a little creative freedom as there was no uniform but the rules were strict, nonetheless.

Once dressed we were taught how to look after our complexion; how to apply and remove make-up and reminded that such training would stand us in good stead thirty or forty years later. And how right they were! We were also shown how to pack purchases in tissue paper; fold them carefully and pack them into Harrods' wonderful, monogrammed boxes in green with gold lettering. We were also told to open an account at Harrods Bank, the royal bank of Coutts into which our salaries would be paid, and we would receive a 25 percent discount on anything we bought in the store.

Another condition for employment was to attend a college evening class at Charing Cross, a long way across town, one night a week after closing time. This covered different areas; amongst them the proper way to display products in the store, and also the matter of the quality of materials we would work with; something I'd never thought of before. Harrods' buyers were experts in every field and we even had a complete department specializing solely in Scottish tartans. We were shown how to distinguish everything between inferior and top quality cottons and the fabrics which were used for evening wear including silks, satins and velvets.

After three or four weeks of training, each newcomer was allocated her department and mine was designer dresses. Here my boss was the buyer, Miss Lucas, and she had a secretary and two full-time sales ladies. The dresses she bought in from London's many fashion houses were hugely expensive and displayed in the department before being tried on by her customers, most of whom were very rich indeed and often had a full-time account at the store.

The fittings took place in big luxurious rooms lit with chandeliers and furnished with exquisite tables and chairs, and one of my first jobs was to bring teas and coffees to our clients and carry dresses to and from the rooms. Often alterations were necessary and once the saleswoman had made the adjustments with measurements and pins another job for me was to take them to the alteration room back in the basement. Down below you could find people of all races, colours and creeds but back then, regrettably, only white people were allowed to serve in the main store.

I was also discreetly informed about Harrods' window-dressers who created the fantastic designs that were the store's displays to a wondering world. We were told that these men were somehow 'different', and of course they were gay, but nothing more was said, and my new work colleagues didn't seem 'different' to me at all.

Miss Lucas and I became friendly. She was a knowledgeable sophisticated woman, very smart and in her forties. Later on I would go with her to London's legendary fashion houses; beautiful Georgian mansions all over the West End but often with quite unobtrusive entrances away from the main streets. We always travelled in taxis; a first for me. And once inside, along with buyers from Selfridge's, Gamages, Debenham's, Fortnum and Mason, Bourne and Hollingsworth and Harvey Nichols (later the favourite shopping destination for Diana Princess of Wales), we watched super-slim models parade their wares: beautiful, and priceless creations from London's top fashion designers: Hardy Amess, Norman Hartnell (who was the Queen's personal designer), Molyneux and Victor Stiebel. Sometimes Miss Lucas would send me on my own to collect a dress from one of the houses but this time the trip was by bus and only after I had collected my precious cargo, was I told, equally firmly, that I must travel back to the store by taxi. I also started to cover the department when my fellow saleswomen went to lunch and so, one fantastic day, made my first personal sale: a simple enough day dress costing around £400. But today this sum would total almost £8000.00.

CHAPTER SIXTEEN

During 1961 whilst at Harrods I'd applied for a student nursing position in three different hospitals. I attended all three interviews and as I'd passed GCEs in human biology, chemistry, physiology and hygiene I could choose where to start my nursing career. So, I decided on Rochford in Essex. This small market town would allow me to be fairly close to some of my Ilford friends and the bike ride of thirty-five miles wouldn't take long. But I would have to wait until I was eighteen in March 1962.

My time at Harrods had been a revelation and I'd seen London at a time when it was just starting to swing at the tail-end of the once-famous 'Season'. This had pertained for two hundred years previously (Julian Slade's musical *Salad Days* which opened in 1954 and ran for over two thousand performances was still quite happy to talk about 'the Season' in its score and plot). But less than ten years after *Salad Days* came huge fashion changes as the sixties dawned amid what may have been the biggest Renaissance of all in popular culture. I remember walking down Brompton Road and seeing my first 'Biba' shop in Knightsbridge; then Mary Quant as I made my way along Kings Road Chelsea and into Carnaby Street watching fashions change forever before my eyes. The teenage market and Britain's youthquake had arrived; Quant's miniskirts, pioneered by Lesley Hornby — now known over the world as 'Twiggy' — had appeared by 1966 and nothing would ever be the same again. I loved miniskirts; they were sexy and offered freedom so you could move faster in them even though the tights remained. Gradually too the changes would filter through to the grand old fashion houses I'd visited before. Ladies' hemlines started to rise too and even prim shy Aunt Jessie thought it was all right to show more than an ankle.

I was enjoying the swinging sixties immensely — and London — and knew that I would miss them both. But my mind was made up. When I handed my months' notice into Miss Lucas, she seemed genuinely disappointed; asked me to reconsider and told me that I had a bright future ahead of me at Harrods. But I stuck to my decision. Aunt Mary was sad to see her lodger move on too; but I kissed her and Uncle Jim goodbye for now and told them I'd be back soon.

So, in April 1961 with all my worldly possessions in a suitcase borrowed from Mary, I took the train to Rochford and enrolled as a student nurse. For now I would be living in the nurses' home but that was fine; I had a big room all to myself and access, at last, to a very large bathroom of which I made full and luxurious daily use. I'd brought my trusted bike with me too so I could get to know the beautiful flat Essex countryside around Rochford, the total rural opposite to Ilford or Canning Town.

I took to nursing from the start but the hours were long; night-time shifts ran from eight in the evening to eight in the morning, and what there was of my monthly salary usually ran out after about a week; there was nothing to spend on treats or luxuries and only hospital food, basic to say the best, to keep us going. I was still listening to music, especially jazz — and began to ask if anyone knew of live jazz anywhere locally? There had been plenty in Ilford and London but finding some in Southend took some doing. But I managed it and was able to introduce some of my new nursing colleagues to the music, some of them for the first time. But there was always that ten-o-clock curfew in the nurses' home.

When I was working the night shift at Rochford, it was normal for most students to sleep the day away. But after a few weeks, I found that I was going to bed later and later and finally gave up going to bed at all. For three clear days and nights I saw friends, cycled for miles, listened to all the jazz there was and led two lives for the price of one. But this couldn't last forever. When my fling was over, I slept for thirty-six straight hours, missing my shifts and gaining a round reprimand from a stern-faced matron.

After the first year, we were allowed to live outside the nurses' home so a fellow student, Angie and I decided to share a small bedsit. I found one in Southend and we moved in. This was much more fun; we could get back home later at night if we'd been out to see a film or listen to music. Our new pad was tiny but as the two of us regularly worked different hospital shifts this didn't matter too much. Otherwise, it could become a little crowded. One night I came back with a friend to find Angie curled up fast asleep on the bed with her boyfriend Dave; the makings, I suppose, of a friendly foursome but nothing happened.

My new flatmate wasn't always practical however, and one day she left a damp towel draped across a paraffin heater. Luckily, I came back home soon after and found the whole flat full of black smoke and smelling awful. It was a big clean-up job; the smoke had penetrated everywhere so soon after we decided to fly solo and find separate flats of our own.

The winter of 1962–3 was the coldest I'd ever known. This was Britain's legendary 'Big Freeze'; one of the worst on record. Temperatures plummeted; lakes and rivers began to freeze over, and so we were told, (I was never sure how they knew), only the winters of 1683–4 and 1739–40 had been colder. Snow fell early in January and piled up in the streets making it almost impossible to get about without slipping or falling over, and Rochford hospital was quickly full of patients with broken ankles, legs and arms. The local council eventually managed to pile the snow up in big mounds which stood like icy statues on pavements for three months before they gradually melted away. At one stage even the whole of the salt-water Thames Estuary froze over from Essex to Kent. Waiting for buses was a long business, and for the first time, I developed chilblains on both my ankles. So I took to walking as fast as possible to keep my circulation moving and bought my first pair of zip-up boots. I also began to think that it would be nice to drive to work in a warm car, but no hope of that; my student nurse's salary wouldn't even lay down a deposit.

So, after two years I decided that enough was enough; a car was now a necessity. Finding a position with a better salary was essential, so I applied for a job with the Robert Seligman Corporation, based in London in Berkeley Square.

Seligman's company specialised in women's hair and beauty salons, and from its beginnings in the USA he was expanding his organization into Europe and now mainland Britain, opening multi-purpose outlets all over the UK. By the late 1960s he was recognized as a true pioneer in women's' fashion; in charge of the largest salon chain of hairdressers in the world and riding the crest of a whole new era in women's hairdressing. In this, he was a near-contemporary to the legendary Vidal Sassoon who had trained in Mayfair and opened his first salon in 1954 in London where his revolutionary creations included the geometric cut and 'Nancy Kwan' hairstyles. Ten years later he would create his signature style; angular and cut on a horizontal plane. This was the 1960s redefinition of the classic 'bob cut' which had been around for forty years, and the revolution would take him to New York where he opened his first salon, on Madison Avenue in 1965.

Sassoon's new sleek look included blow-drying: relegating the venerable 'shampoo and set with curlers' style to a thing of the past. The cut of a woman's hair was now the new priority; hair salons were being forced to move with the times and this was what I would be employed to do. So, after an interview with a representative, Robert Seligman and his corporation decided that I would be right for the job and found me a post at Keddie's department store in Southend High Street. Later I would move out to the whole of East Anglia as an area manager opening new salons; a job which involved everything from installing tills to finding uniforms. Then there was the matter of staff; recruitment to begin with, then training to make sure that every new member was qualified to work on the floor and sometimes bringing in specialists to retrain existing staff who were falling behind the new times.

So now I was earning that much-needed better salary, had my own flat and started intensive driving lessons. My instructor would call for me at seven-thirty in the morning, and I'd take an hour's instruction before work, then another after the salon closed. This arrangement continued at full speed until it was time to take my driving test. The day came, but it was snowing and there was talk of cancellation but after an hour or two we got started and I slithered along the icy road taking great care. I'm sure that my steady driving helped me pass the test. And while taking lessons I'd been saving every last penny and found enough money for some sort of second-hand car.

Within a week or two I had my very first set of wheels. During my lessons I'd been driving a new Ford Fiesta, but now all I could afford was an ageing Morris Minor which had probably made its debut at Britain's 1948 Motor Show. It got me to and fro and was inexpensive to run. But it was a surprise when I was stopped by a police car one day and told that I had exceeded the speed limit of 30mph in a one way system.

"Really?" I said. "In this car? Impossible surely!"

But I avoided getting a ticket. Maybe he liked the look of me and my ancient vehicle.

I was fed up with the Morris anyhow but saving for a better car would take far too long, so I decided to try for a loan at Barclays bank. This was quite an ambitious move; back at that time women seldom applied for bank loans, but I was young, healthy and cheeky and thought it was worth a try. The bank manager raised his eyebrows but I had him cornered; a regular salary paid into my account and my old Morris as part exchange against a better car. So, I got my loan and agreed to pay it back in a year. But the debt was settled in six months and my next car was a sporty Ford Anglia no more than two years old; decidedly nippy, and I could fill up the tank for a week for no more than four pounds.

Because of long working hours and staying away from home for overnight stays in East Anglia while working for Seligman's, I wasn't able to see so much of my aunts now. But once again faithful Jessie was the exception. Our company had opened a branch in Romford, close to Ilford where Jessie still lived at 251 Kingston Road. So, I would arrange to call and see her when business was over.

Jessie was always pleased to see me, but by now husband Albert had died and she was lonely. She had never quite caught up to the twentieth century and affectionate stories of her eccentricities were circulating among her sisters and on down to me. At one point after lengthy deliberation and negotiation, she had decided to exchange her gas cooker with one from a neighbour several streets away. Brother Jimmy had disconnected the cooker, carried it out of the kitchen, loaded it into a wheelbarrow and begun the long trip down the road with Jessie alongside carrying on the cleaning with a brush. Then out of the blue — and halfway to its new destination — she changed her mind and the stove had to be returned to its old home.

She was worried about the dangers of electricity too; even a new electric kettle was not to be trusted, and suspicious of its switch and lead, she would continue to use her favourite whistling predecessor on her old stove's hob. The gift of a fridge from the family was similarly rejected and she continued to keep her milk in the stone cooler she had always used. An electric vacuum cleaner was definitely out of the question too, and to the end of her days, she would use the trusted all-acoustic carpet cleaner called Ewbank. One more electric device which she reluctantly allowed — but had her suspicions about — was the two-bar electric fire she kept in her living room. When visitors arrived, she would hospitably turn the fire on; then after ten minutes or so query 'isn't it rather hot in here?' and turn it off again. As the room cooled down, she would change her mind and turn it back on, so that if you were there for an hour's visit the fire might be turned on and off half a dozen times.

But although Jessie was becoming an eccentric elderly woman, I knew that she had always been good in a crisis, and still trusted her unerring sense of judgment. Her unobtrusive presence had been there all along from my earliest memories; to care for my mother at Kingston Road; to find a housekeeper for James; to watch over me and my childhood tomboy years and to put me right where necessary. Later when my father had knocked my head through the glass door panel, she had been there to rescue me and save our family's reputation with a lie.

Then one day Jessie said to me. "Why don't you go and see him?"

"Who do you mean Auntie?" I asked.

"Your father," she said.

CHAPTER SEVENTEEN

I wondered about my aunt's suggestion but I hadn't seen my father for over twenty years. The anger and hurt after his assault had waned over time, but I really had no wish to make the short walk back to 165 Kingston Road where all the good memories had been erased and now only bad ones remained. With the help of Jessie and her five sisters I had made my way in the world too; lost my cockney accent, enjoyed happy holidays as well as education at a fine school and become confident in my social skills. Now I was running a high-powered job in women's fashion, making money for myself and happy in my own skin. So why go back?

The only contact from my father over the years had been his annual birthday card. I always recognised his handwriting on the envelope when it came through the letterbox as, like many left-handed people over the years, he had been forced by unthinking teachers to write with his right. But beyond that, there had been nothing. Brother Jimmy had long been away from home; he had been called up, then married and would barely go back to Ilford at all. By now there had been more in-family strife between my father and stepson Graham who, as a result, had gone to live in Australia. And the daughter James had fathered with Rose would be in her teens and the apple of her mother's eye; presumably, she was now the daughter he wanted to care for too, and any love he had for me was long gone. There had been no telephone call or letter either and I had begun to presume that I was now just a part of his past. I was busy too; the shabby sad atmosphere at 165 Kingston Road was long gone and probably, I thought, I would never see my father again. And perhaps I didn't want to. But Aunt Jessie felt differently.

These days our visits were far more formalised. I would have to write to her to arrange a meeting as she still had no telephone and refused to answer the door if she didn't know who was waiting outside. But every time I'd visit, once inside we would talk and Jessie, as always, would want to know all about what I was doing, and tell me about what my other five aunts were doing too. There would be a cup of tea and reminiscences about my childhood years; my mother, and how the two of them had been so close; about dear Albert, his fruity cough and how the smoking had finally brought him down, and any small problems she had as a lonely widow.

And then Jessie would start to talk about my father again; when she had last seen him down the road, about stepmother Rose and their daughter too and why hadn't I paid a visit yet? This was completely unlike my aunt's normal way of thinking, speaking or acting. But she wanted a reunion and gradually her queries became more persistent. But still, I wasn't sure. Did I want to revisit my old unhappy home? Or would the door even be opened to me should I make the effort?

But I wanted to please my aunt and perhaps — just perhaps — it was time to try. There were forty-two neat, terraced houses between Jessie's and my old home, but they represented much more than the few hundred yards it would take to walk the distance. So taking the wheel behind my snappy Ford Anglia, I turned the ignition key, drove the short way down the road that Jessie had traversed thousands of times and parked up to look at the old house. It still looked much the same but now it was I who had made the changes, steering my life into a new world. And none of them had been prompted by the two people who still lived behind the old dark green door. But what was going on behind it? An old rock and roll song crossed my musical mind.

But at last, I walked up the short path to the front door and lifted the knocker. This was the biggest step I'd taken in my family's life, and in the silence that followed, I thought about turning away. But after a short pause though I heard steps in the hall and my stepmother opened the door. Now she looked older and as she looked at me her face remained expressionless. But though she said nothing the door stayed ajar and I heard her call out to James.

"There's someone here to see you."

And then, there was my father. He appeared at the front door almost as if nothing had happened. But his welcoming arms were open as if to say, 'I'm glad you're here' and his greeting was simple.

"Come on in and have a cup of tea."

After twenty years was this all he could say? So it seemed, so in I went, and my father and I exchanged our first tentative words while Rose made a point of keeping out of the way. There was no mention at all of our traumatic parting and we talked about the usual things; how I was, how he was, and what he had been doing. It turned out that my father had gone back to sea after Beckton Gas Works closed down, joining his brother John on the old Port Line. But recently he had retired and he and Rose had finally bought their house after their landlady had grown too old to collect the rent. Apart from that, it was almost as if nothing had ever happened. Gradually the conversation eased and as my visits continued Rose would float in and out of the room, feeling her way back into the remnants of a relationship.

Gradually my father and I got to know each other again too. By now he had aged but still liked to laugh and joke and to drink, though now his capacity for alcohol had reduced first to a pint of Guinness, then just the half. His loud cockney voice and ways were more fun again, and in a pub his resonant query 'where can I get a jimmy-riddle?' caused heads to turn and smile, just as they had done when his big throaty voice called out to neighbours as we rode together through Ilford on his bicycle all those years ago.

But he had always been a tightwad too. When my brother Jim had married, James had bought him an Ascot heater but refused to have one in the house himself as he was sure they used too much gas. And on one late visit to his last home in Eastwood Essex, I arrived at the house to hear that he was in the garage. So down the garden I went to meet him and found him hard at work with three clocks nearby. As we left, he began methodically to remove their batteries and I asked why.

"Well," said my father. "I don't need to leave them in the clocks when I'm not down here. It uses all the power up." It was hard not to love him again.

For most of his life, James Sweetingham had done all the wrong things — smoking, drinking and eating whatever he liked, but he would live until he was eighty-eight defying all of nature's most threatening rules. Later after we knew each other well again, he was most concerned to remind me that he had saved enough money for his own funeral. But meantime the six sisters, who were my aunts, had helped me to grow up, to forgive him and to move on.

Envoi.

It had been Aunt Jessie who had prompted me into making the hardest reconciliation of my life. But in the meantime my faithful aunt had done one more thing for me that not one of her five remaining sisters could find it in their hearts to do.

At the age of nineteen, young, full of fire and with a successful career running at top speed, I had fallen in love with a married man, thirteen years my senior, and we had begun an affair. Only two of my aunts knew and one of them was Mary who wrote to me with a letter saying flatly 'this must stop'. But Jessie, as ever, was there for me. One day she travelled from Kingston Road to Southend — a big journey for a shy elderly woman — to talk gently about what had happened; the pitfalls of the situation; that a married man very often returned to his wife after the affair, and that I could be badly hurt in the process. Worst of all she reminded me, I could have a baby too. But she was the only one of my six aunts to care about what might happen to me. And after my lover had become my permanent partner — and husband for forty more years — she would visit us again to once again become part of a new and happy family.

So, what happened to Jessie? After Albert died it took her a long time to make the final move from 251 Kingston Road once a comfortable home but now riddled with rising damp and little more than a wreck.

When she finally did it was to a flat in Chadwell Heath five miles away on a snowy midwinter day. But although her sisters had already done most of her packing, Jessie really didn't want to move at all. I had gone down the night before to help her finish the job, only to find that my poor aunt had unpacked everything again. When at last we arrived at her new home, she didn't want me to leave and caught hold of my arm to try and keep me with her.

For her remaining years Jessie would live in her first-floor flat; she was less likely, she felt, to be burgled upstairs. Any caller, including me, would have to make a call (at long last she had had a telephone installed), and specify a time of arrival or she wouldn't answer the door.

She became more obsessive about burglary and her cash was kept in her flat so in the end, there was no need to go out to the bank at all.

I continued to visit but later on, when I moved to Spain for a while with my husband, my loving aunt missed me and while I was away her health deteriorated and she was moved into a geriatric ward. On one last visit she recognised my father but not me. Soon after, bandbox fresh and upright in her coat, matching hat and gloves, my Aunt Jessie would float away gently to meet Albert and whatever maker she had espoused.

She was the longest lasting influence of my life and one of seven remarkable sisters; different flowers from one garden who between them birthed me, mothered me and brought me to womanhood.

Call thyself sister, sweet, for I am thee.
Thee will I love and with thee lead my life.
William Shakespeare — *The Comedy of Errors*, 1594